D0585863

TEA CULTURE

Created by Penn Publishing Ltd.
Design: Michal & Dekel
Layout: Neta Shoham
Culinary editor: Tal Aniv-Bregman

Published by Imagine Publishing, Inc.
25 Whitman Road, Morganville, NJ 07751
and Penn Publishing Ltd.
1 Yehuda Halevi Street, Tel Aviv, Israel 65135

Distributed in the United States by BookMasters Distribution Services, Inc.
30 Amberwood Parkway, Ashland, OH 44805

Distributed in Canada by BookMasters Distribution Services
c/o Jacqueline Gross Associates, 165 Dufferin Street
Toronto, Ontario, Canada M6K 3H6

Distributed in the United Kingdom by Publishers Group UK
8 The Arena, Mollison Avenue, Enfield, EN3 7NL, UK

Library of Congress Cataloging-in-Publication Data

Dubrin, Beverly.
Tea culture / Beverly Dubrin.
          p. cm.
Includes index.
ISBN 978-1-936140-05-3
1. Tea. 2. Tea—History. 3. Cookery (Tea) I. Title.
 TX817.T3D826 2010
641.3'372—dc22
                              2009032675
2 4 6 8 10 9 7 5 3 1

For information about custom editions, special sales, premium and corporate purchases, please
contact Imagine Publishing, Inc. at specialsales@imaginebks.com

Tea culture

Beverly Dubrin

Penn/imagine!
Publishing
New York
www.imaginebks.com

Contents

....

Introduction

My first tea memory is of my Russian-born grandmother sitting at her kitchen table, sipping a glass of hot tea. As I was growing up, I remember my mother chatting with friends in the living room, while eating cookies and sipping tea from bone china cups. My mother so treasured her cup and saucer collection that, for birthdays and other special occasions, my father and I would shop for yet another set for her. I cherish what remains of Mother's bone china, using it when friends come for special visits.

It was not until I went away to college that tea became an essential part of my life. Every afternoon my dormitory housemother would brew a pot of orange and sweet, spice-flavored black tea and open her apartment door, inviting us to stop in for a visit and a cup of tea. The aroma of the tea was so intoxicating that I couldn't resist taking a few minutes for a cup, almost every day. These regular visits provided me with the opportunity to relax and to build a trusting friendship with my housemother and classmates, who also welcomed the brief respite from academic stress. To this day, I associate this fragrant tea with cozy surroundings and special friendships. I always have a box of it on my tea shelf.

Today, tea is a part of my daily routine. I start my workday with a steaming cup of citrus green tea, which I sip slowly as I work at my computer. As my day progresses, I consume several more cups of tea, selecting different types and flavors to suit my mood, the weather, and the time of day. My day ends with an after-dinner cup of herbal infusion or decaffeinated tea. When a friend or associate stops by, the first thing I ask is, "Would you like a cup of tea?" A simple cup of tea sets the stage for a leisurely visit.

Previous page: A group of 'nippies', waitresses from a J. Lyons teahouse, 1981.

Tea plays an important part in contemporary culture. There are tearooms and tea cafés in most major cities. Many hotels provide an afternoon tea service. Cruise ships serve daily afternoon tea. One international social organization, which started in Fullerton, California, has regular tea outings, Its members, all women of a "certain age", dress up in red hats and purple attire on each occasion. Having a tea party is a popular way to celebrate birthdays, bridal and baby showers, and other special occasions. It is not surprising to find dozens of different kinds of tea on the kitchen shelves of tea drinkers. We drink tea both formally and informally.

Tea has come a long way from the simple black variety that my grandmother and mother sipped. Our tea choices come in many colors and shapes. Of course, our growing interest in tea has given way to an entire industry dedicated to tea accessories.

Tea is said to offer health benefits that coffee and other beverages do not provide. And we don't necessarily have to drink tea to enjoy its benefits, since tea is now an ingredient in foods, fragrances, candy, and skin and hair care products.

Join me for a visit and a cup of tea. 🍵

THE WORLD OF TEA

·······

A Brief History of the Discovery of Tea

A popular legend about the discovery of tea as a beverage dates back to about 2700 BC in China. According to the story, Emperor Shen Nung was drinking a cup of boiled water. The Emperor, concerned about hygiene, always insisted that water be boiled before he drank it. Some leaves from a nearby tree fell into his cup, turning the water a deep shade of brown. The color intrigued the Emperor, and he decided to drink the brownish water. Shen Nung was an advocate of herbal medicine, so this wasn't the first time he had tasted something made from a plant. He had been suffering from aches and pains, but after this new 'brown' tea he felt refreshed, energetic, and pain-free.

The tea tree, or plant, *Camellia Sinensis*, is indigenous to China, India, and other parts of Southeast Asia. However, little is known about the use of tea anywhere outside China until sometime in the sixth century, when legends tell of the discovery of tea in other parts of world.

In one such legend, the Indian Prince Bhodidharma, who was known in China as Ta-mo and in Japan as Daruma, traveled from South India to China to preach Buddhism. An advocate of meditation, the Prince vowed to meditate, without sleeping, for nine years (seven, in another version). He kept it up for five years, but then became sleepy, so he absent-mindedly picked a few leaves from a nearby tree and chewed them. This was a tea tree and the leaves gave him the energy he needed to fulfill his meditation vow. Prince Bhodidharma's practice of meditating for long periods, while drinking tea to remain alert, is said to be the foundation of Zen Buddhism.

A popular variation on Prince Bhodidharma's story is that the Prince fell asleep after three years of meditation and dreamt about the women he had once loved. When he awoke, he was so distraught at having fallen asleep that he tore off his eyelids and buried them in the dirt, vowing to never sleep again. Some time later, he returned to this spot and discovered an unknown bush growing just on the spot where he had buried his eyelids. He picked a few leaves from the bush, chewed on them, and felt a surge of energy. Fascinated by the powers of the tea leaves, the Prince shared his discovery with his followers, offering them seeds from his tea bush. When he moved on to Japan to further advocate Buddhism, he brought tea bush seeds with him.

The Chinese continued to drink tea for the medicinal and energizing effects that Emperor Shen Nung had discovered. Sometime in the Period of Disunity (AD 220–589), the Chinese invented a process to remove some of the bitterness of brewed tea. They also began steaming the tea leaves and compressing them into solid bricks.

During the Tang Dynasty (AD 618–907), Japanese Buddhist monks began bringing tea bricks back with them when they returned from their missionary visits to China. Tea drinking became associated with sophistication. Teahouses and tea gardens sprang up. During this time, the scholar Lu Yu wrote the first book about tea, *The Classic of Tea*, a treatise on the history of tea and the art of producing, brewing and drinking tea. *The Classic of Tea* is still read today. By the time the Song Dynasty began (AD 960–1279), tea was well integrated into Chinese and Japanese culture. Tea was no longer an exclusive beverage, reserved for royalty and the wealthy. Ordinary citizens gathered in teahouses to enjoy tea, tea snacks, and the company of friends. Special cups and pots for tea were created, marking the beginning of teaware.

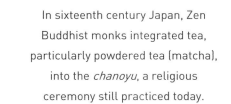

In sixteenth century Japan, Zen Buddhist monks integrated tea, particularly powdered tea (matcha), into the *chanoyu*, a religious ceremony still practiced today.

Opposite: Tea cakes are set out for visitors to the gardens of Daichiji Temple, near Kyoto, Kansai Triangle, Honshu Island, Japan.

Tea culture languished during Mongol Kublai Kahn's Yuan Dynasty (AD 1271–1368). Tea remained a desired commodity, but little occurred to advance its place in Chinese culture. It was during the Ming Dynasty (AD 1368–1644) that progress was made in the processing of tea, and tea drinking returned as an integral part of Chinese social culture. The oxidation process was perfected and production techniques were developed.

These same techniques are used in the production of the teas we drink today. During the Manchu, or Qing, Dynasty (AD 1644–1911), the Chinese continued to consume tea, in both the refined and plebeian ways of earlier dynasties. The important development during this period was the tea trade, in which Chinese tea was transported to regions throughout the Far East.

Tea also made its way to Europe at this time. In 1560, a Portuguese missionary named Father Jasper de Cruz sampled tea while on a mission to China. His discovery led to the emergence of tea in the rest of the world. However, it was the Dutch, rather than the Portuguese, who turned the European tea trade into big business. As early as 1610, Chinese tea was being shipped to Holland. By the mid-1600s, it was being shipped to the American Dutch colony, New Amsterdam (New York).

Tea became more popular than coffee and cocoa in London coffeehouses. The coffeehouses were known as "penny universities" because for a penny, customers (men only at the time) could obtain a pot of tea and a newspaper. These coffeehouses were not just gathering places for scholars and intellectuals. With their modest prices, they were social centers for everyone, from modest shopkeepers to wealthy gentlemen. In addition to the reading of newspapers, there was an abundance of

Tea is second to water as the most-consumed beverage in the world.

Opposite: An English family having morning tea in Simla, India, 1871.

lively conversation and gossip. The London coffeehouses of the second half of the seventeenth century functioned much like cafés today; a place to chat to friends, hold a business meeting, or catch up on the latest news in the neighborhood. Of course, there was no Internet access back then and probably no takeout cups, but they served pretty much the same purpose as today. In 1662 King Charles II of England married Portuguese Princess Catherine of Braganza, who was an avid tea drinker. In spite of this, women remained excluded from coffeehouses—the only public places to drink tea. Things changed in 1717, when Thomas Twining opened a teashop, the Golden Lyon, which provided loose-leaf tea for his thriving enterprise next door, Tom's Coffee House.

Women flocked to the Golden Lyon to purchase tea to brew at home. Customers could sip cups of brewed tea in the shop, ostensibly to sample it before making a purchase. With access to tea, Englishwomen started hosting tea parties at home. Home tea parties, to which men were often invited, evolved into high society gatherings, while coffeehouses lost their exclusivity as social gathering places. Mr. Twining deserves his place in history as a visionary businessman; Twinings of London continues to thrive today, selling tea in more than 100 countries throughout the world. The English became so enchanted with tea that they stopped importing it through the Dutch trading companies and set up their own—the English East India Company. Up until 1834, when tea trade with China was opened to competition, the English East India Company was the exclusive importer of tea to England.

Meanwhile, in America, the British colonies were becoming resentful of the taxes imposed on tea and other commodities shipped from England. In protest, they boycotted English tea. The Boston Tea Party, on December 16, 1773, was the

Opposite: A genteel tea party at Thorne Road in Doncaster, Yorkshire, England.

colonists' response to British demands to accept the tea. They dumped the cargo from three ships, about 120,000 pounds of tea, into Boston Harbor. Tea-dumping protests took place in other American cities in subsequent months, and the colonists went from being avid tea drinkers to rejecting tea entirely. The Boston Tea Party was a significant event, which led to the American Revolution.

While the Boston Tea Party ended England's tea trade with America, it did not diminish England's demand for tea from China. The ever-growing popularity of tea in England actually increased its demand for tea. However, England lacked either the money with which to purchase tea from the Chinese, or the products that the Chinese demanded in exchange for the tea. Eventually, the British did find one item that interested the Chinese—opium. Opium grew in India, which was part of the British Empire. As the British "addiction" to tea grew, the Chinese developed a true addiction to opium. When opium addiction reached what was deemed an intolerable level, the Chinese attempted to totally eliminate the drug from the country. The Opium Wars (1839–1842) that developed between the British and the Chinese went deeper than the issue of opium. For decades, the British had been trying to convince the Chinese to open up free trade with Britain and the rest of the Western world. When the Treaty of Nanking was signed in 1942, Hong Kong became a British colony. As a result, Chinese ports were opened to free trade and the British were compensated for the destroyed opium. The Opium Wars did little to diminish the Chinese demand for opium. Opium trade was legalized between 1858 and 1917, at which time China was producing enough of its own opium to eliminate the need for imports from India. During this period England became less dependent on China for tea by developing its own tea production in its colonies.

To this day, every December 16, starting at the Old South Meeting House and continuing out onto Boston Harbor, a group called the Old South's Tea Party Players reenacts the Boston Tea Party.

Opposite: The Boston Tea Party. Reproduction based on engraving by D. Berger, 1784, after D. Chodowiecki, circa 1903.

„BOSTON TEA-PARTY.“

Three cargoes of tea distroyed. Dec. 16. 1773.

A number of the inhabitants, disguised as Indians, boarded the ships in the night, broke open all the chests of tea, and emptied the contents into the sea.

Today, tea is cultivated throughout the world—in China, Japan, India, Africa, Indonesia, Sri Lanka, Australia, as well as in countries in the Middle East, South America, South Pacific, and Southeast Asia. Experimentation in tea cultivation continues. In the U.S. small tea plantations operate in South Carolina and Hawaii.

The oldest wild tea plant in the world is said to be more than 3,200 years old. It is on the Mountain of Fragrant Bamboo, near Xiaowan in China's Yunnan Province.

Tea Rituals and Ceremonies

The most elaborate tea ceremony is the Japanese Zen Buddhist *Chanoyu*—"the way of tea"—which dates back to the sixteenth century. Tea master Sen Rikyu developed this version of the tea ceremony, which is still practiced and studied by Zen monks and tea scholars today. The general philosophy behind *chanoyu* is that the spirit, man, and nature come together in a serene setting, in which knowledge can grow into wisdom. Participants experience the four principles of an enlightened life: tranquility, purity, harmony, and respect. This ceremony of ritualized hospitality centers around the drinking of individually prepared cups of a powdered green tea called *matcha*. Each serving is measured out with a tea scoop (*chashaku*), whisked with a bamboo whisk (*chasen*), and served in a tea bowl (*chawan*). A special linen or hemp cloth (*chakin*) is used to wipe the tea bowl.

For the *chanoyu*, the host traditionally wears a kimono. Guests wear kimonos or conservative clothing. They remove their shoes before entering the teahouse, usually a building used exclusively for the *chanoyu*. The floor of the tearoom is covered with woven straw mats (*tatami*). Guests sit on the *tatami* in a seiza style—on their knees, leaning back on their haunches and heels. Guests are seated in order of prestige, with the honored guest closest to the host.

The *chanoyu* tearoom decor is simple. The host often creates a floral arrangement (*chabana*) from seasonal blossoms picked fresh from a nearby garden. The arrangement is placed in a container made of natural materials. The host often builds a fire in the tearoom for heating the water. Guests may be served a complete meal or some small sweets. Each guest has a special paper (*kaishi*), from which to eat the sweets.

In some *chanoyu*, all guests sip from the same bowl of tea. Starting with the guest of honor, it is passed from one to another with a bow and a few words. In other *chanoyu*, each guest receives a bowl of tea and the bowls are passed in the identical order of priority. Each bowl is passed with the front facing the guest who is receiving it. The recipient then rotates the bowl before sipping, so as to not sip from the front.

Each time the *chanoyu* utensils are cleaned, according to a traditional procedure, they are arranged in order of use for the next ceremony. The guest of honor asks the host to allow the guests to examine the utensils, many of which are irreplaceable antiques. While the guests handle and examine the utensils, one by one, they also meditate and contemplate. After the guests leave the teahouse, the *chanoyu* host bows from the doorway to signal the end of the ceremony. While the Japanese *chanoyu* is the most ritualized of tea ceremonies, the tea-drinking customs of other countries have also become tradition.

If you dine in a Moroccan restaurant anywhere in the world, chances are that dessert will be accompanied by a cup of hot green tea, flavored with spearmint and sugar. The preferred Moroccan tea is Chinese gunpowder green, which is traditionally served in a glass. At the start of the Moroccan tea ceremony, the utensils—a silver teapot with a long spout, a brass hammer to break chunks of sugar from a tall sugar cone, and silver boxes of tea, mint, and sugar cubes—are all set out on a low round table. The ingredients are steeped in boiling water. Each guest has three glasses, into which the tea is poured. The pot is raised high above the glass while pouring. This is not only for effect, but also to aerate the tea, and it results in a bit of froth on top of the tea. Guests are served one glass of tea at a time, throughout the course of the meal. With each subsequent glass of tea, more water and sugar are added to the pot, but no more tea.

Opposite: Two Japanese girls demonstrating the Chanoyu *or tea drinking ceremony, circa 1900s.*

The first glass is said to be bitter, like life, the second glass is like sweet, like love, and the third glass is gentle, like death. According to one legend, the reason for raising the pot while pouring is to show off the mark of the silversmith who crafted it.

In old world Russia, tea was sipped from a glass. In Russian households, the water was kept hot in a large cauldron called a samovar. A small teapot was perched on top of the samovar to keep it warm. The tea was prepared, according to taste, by immersing it in the hot water. To sweeten their tea, Russians sipped it through a sugar cube held in their mouths or stirred a spoonful or two of raspberry jam into their cups.

The centuries-old afternoon tea tradition established by the British is the model for today's tea celebrations. The Tea Socializing chapter elaborates further on afternoon tea as both a social event and a meal. Traditionally, the British either add milk to their tea, or add tea to a few drops of milk. The ritual of 'milk first' is said to create a smooth blend of milk and tea, while that of 'milk last' is said to cool the tea slightly for easier sipping and prevent damaging the leaves with extremely hot water. Some believe that the order in which milk is added to the cup is an indication of social class. The working classes added their milk first, while the upper classes added it after the tea had been poured. According to speculation, the lower classes could not afford high quality porcelain cups, and pouring the milk in first prevented lesser quality earthenware cups from cracking. Whatever the method, it is best to add milk to strong black teas, since it seems to mellow out some of the tannins and give the tea less of a "bite". Adding milk to tea of all colors is regaining popularity, especially in today's tea latte drinks. Another variation is Tibetan yak butter, made from yak milk blended into tea. While most non-Tibetans don't care for yak tea, it is something that visitors "must try".

In most Chinese restaurants, waiters bring a complimentary pot of jasmine tea to the table. Visit a Thai restaurant, and Thai iced tea is probably included in the beverage menu. Modern-day tea rituals are less rigid and formal than those of the past. Many of us simply drink tea throughout the day as an energizing and comforting beverage. We do, however, incorporate tea into special tea parties and celebrations. High tea, low tea, afternoon tea, Teddy Bear tea, and Mad Hatter tea, are some of the tea celebrations described in the Tea Socializing chapter.

Afternoon tea has evolved into a combination of high and low teas. High tea, once called "meat tea", was originally the main meal of the British lower classes, eaten with the family at home at the end of a long workday. Low tea was a light meal or snack, enjoyed by the British upper classes in the late afternoon to tide them over until their more substantial dinner in the evening. Low tea was often a social event, enjoyed in the company of friends and associates. The distinction between high tea and low tea was also a literal one, based on the kind of table used for serving. High tea was consumed at a high dining room table, while low tea was served in the sitting or living room on a lower side table or cocktail table (also called a coffee table).

Both the Teddy Bear tea and Mad Hatter tea are children's celebrations. Teddy Bear tea is usually a Christmas-season celebration enjoyed by children with their parents, grandparents, and other family members. The children, accompanied by their favorite teddy bear or stuffed animal, dress up in their holiday best and go to a tearoom or hotel for afternoon tea or lunch.

In 1869. Arthur Brooke opened a teashop in Manchester, England that became known for its reliable blends of tea. His company grew when he began selling his tea at wholesale prices to grocers who placed large orders. The business evolved into PG Tips in the 1930s, and the blend is still popular in England.

Opposite: Merchants of the city of Nijni-Novgorod take tea together from a samovar, 1905.

The Mad Hatter tea, inspired by Lewis Carroll's *Alice in Wonderland*, is a popular theme for a children's birthday party, with guests arriving in costume. In contrast to the Teddy Bear tea, the Mad Hatter tea is more of a free-for-all, fun occasion, including games and activities in addition to the tea and food. ☕

Opposite: Tea party at the Fairmont Express Victoria, British Columbia.

How and When Do We Drink Our Tea?

Tea is a beverage that can be enjoyed almost anywhere, at any time of the day. It can be drunk hot or cold. It can be sweetened, flavored, diluted with milk, or simply as it is. It can be unceremoniously sipped from a paper cup covered with a plastic lid, or savored in a china cup, poured from the tea pot in which it is brewed. It can also be accompanied by sweet or savory foods.

Tea drinking, like wine drinking, appeals to people on many different levels. There are no strict rules about drinking tea, and each tea drinker's experience with and approach to tea is unique. Some consume the beverage with no concern for differences in quality or taste. Others are very particular about their choices and devote considerable time to learning about tea and developing their tea-tasting palate. Some people drink tea every day; others have a cup only on special occasions.

Sophisticated tea drinkers are more discriminating about the choices they make and may prefer certain varieties for specific occasions and times of day. Some tea drinkers in this category may have a favorite tea that they always drink. Others may vary their teas throughout the day and are likely to drink several cups a day. They may start their day with a robust black breakfast tea, go on to a green tea until lunchtime, and then switch to a white tea for the afternoon. At dinner or in the evening, an herbal or decaffeinated tea may be their beverage of choice. When they shop for tea, they are open to trying new varieties. In teashops, they will ask the sales staff for advice and suggestions. They usually have several different kinds and brands of tea on their tea shelf and, when serving guests, they will offer a variety of choices.

Opposite: Two attendants with a refreshments trolley, London, England, 1915. This photograph is one in a series taken to illustrate the refreshment services which the Great Western Railway (GWR) provided for its passengers at London's Paddington Station.

While people in this group are more discerning, they are by no means elitists. They are comparable to wine drinkers who have their favorite brands of wine and favorite places to buy it from. Wine drinkers may have a trusted wine merchant with whom they consult when they are shopping for wine for a special occasion. And, after trying the wine that the merchant recommends, they will take the time to return to the shop to share their opinion.

For the most sophisticated tea drinker—the tea expert—tea is a passion. Just as the wine connoisseur travels the world in search of new and obscure varieties, so may the tea aficionado. This group of tea experts seeks out distinctive teas, often exploring particular plantations and specific vintages. They may even conduct comparative tastings, perhaps sampling the same tea from different years, or one from different harvests from the same region. They investigate how different origin, weather, soil, and growing conditions result in variations in the same tea, in much the same way that wine experts track wine vintages from year to year. Tea experts, by profession or hobby, can identify teas, including their origin, in blind taste tests. Professional tea tasters train for as long as four years. Working for tea estates, tea companies, and tea auction houses, they are able to taste up to four hundred samples in a given day.

Tea purists insist that tea brewed from loose, bulk tea is superior to tea brewed from tea bags. With the growing popularity of tea and recent innovations in tea bag design, the premise that loose tea produces a better cup is debatable. Some tea experts have conceded that quality is not a result of how the tea is packaged, but rather the quality of the tea itself and method for brewing it. 🍃

As with wine tasting, there is a protocol for professional tea tasting, and certificates are granted by study and training programs. The title of Tea Master is no longer reserved for the Japanese Buddhist monks who dedicate their lives to mastering the intricacies of the tea ceremony.

Opposite: A young girl pretends to pour her mother a cup of tea while sitting under a Christmas tree with presents on the floor of their living room, 1960s.

Tea Bag Design and Innovation

Salada Tea was founded by Peter C. Larkin, a world traveler and food merchant. " Salada introduced tea bags in the 1930s. For convenient removal after steeping, one end of a string was attached to the tea bag and the other to a paper tag, which remained outside the cup and could be grasped easily to avoid contact with the hot tea. In the early 1960s, Salada added a special feature to its teabags—a few words of wit or wisdom.

Tea bags have come a long way since 1908, when a New York tea merchant, Thomas Sullivan, decided to cut marketing costs by packaging his tea samples in small silk bags, tied at the top with a string, rather than sending full-sized tins for his customers to sample. Mr. Sullivan's customers, not realizing that the bag was simply intended as a convenient receptacle for a small tea sample, treated it as a tea infuser and submerged it in water to brew. This marked the invention of the tea bag.

Before tea bags became available, tea drinkers often used refillable, perforated metal infusers, also called tea balls or tea eggs, which they filled with loose tea and immersed in hot water just like a tea bag. Once the tea had steeped sufficiently, the infusers could be easily and neatly removed. The tea bag made tea accessible to a larger market, since tinned tea was much more expensive.

The tea bag enabled tea drinkers to purchase and brew tea conveniently, with no additional accessories. It has been refined over the years by experimenting with different materials and sealing methods.

The original tea bags were small fabric pouches filled with tea, much like the pouches Mr. Sullivan created for his tea samples. It was not until 1944 that the flat rectangular tea bag, made of porous paper fiber, was invented. This is the tea bag I remember dangling in my Grandma's glass of tea.

Opposite: Shopkeeper arranging Salada tea bags on shelves.

A significant modification of the flat, two-sided tea bag was made in 1952, when the Lipton Tea Company patented its Flo-Thru® tea bag; a four-sided, double-chamber bag that allowed the tea greater contact with the water and more room to expand in the bag. Until recently, tea brewed from bags was considered inferior to tea brewed from loose leaves. This is probably because the less expensive tea bags were often filled with tea that had been crushed to a dusty consistency and deprived of much of its natural oil and flavor. Some say that tea bags were filled with the cuttings that remained after tea processors packaged whole-leaf, loose tea. Others were certain that even if the best whole-leaf tea were packaged in a tea bag, it would not have enough room to expand properly when coming into contact with hot water.

Nevertheless, tea bags became popular throughout most of the world as a convenient way to prepare a cup of tea. Tea bag advocates argue that loose-leaf tea, if packed too tightly into a tea ball or tea infuser, cannot properly expand and will produce an unsatisfactory cup or pot of tea. Tea bags, they say, provide the appropriate quantity of tea for brewing. In addition, they point out that loose tea left in a tea cup or pot beyond the appropriate brewing time (a likely possibility since it is not easily removed) produces overly strong, even bitter, tea. A tea bag can be easily removed when the tea is brewed. An increased interest in tea has given rise to new innovations in tea bags. The traditional flat squares or rectangles are now joined by other shapes, such as circles and pyramids. While the traditional tea bag has a string stapled to its top and a decorative paper label at the end that hangs outside the cup, newer bags have innovative designs for dunking and removing the bag, such as a rigid "stem" that hangs over the rim of the cup. Some tea bags are string-less pouches that float in the water and must be fished out of the bottom of the cup.

Sir Thomas J. Lipton, a Scottish-born entrepreneur, was the first tea manufacturer to buy his own tea estates as a means of ensuring consistently high quality. In 1890, Lipton was the first to sell tea exclusively in prepackaged packages. Lipton Tea continues to be a staple in many households.

Opposite: An advertisement for Lipton's Tea, showing one of their plantations in Ceylon, circa 1860.

While paper fiber is still widely used to manufacture tea bags, tea companies now boast of bags made from organic, recyclable, biodegradable materials. Many top tea companies package their tea in silken fabric tea bags. Today's tea bags are filled with whole-leaf tea, herbs, spices, and dried fruits; in any and all combinations. Modern-day tea bag construction enables the tea to come in full contact with the water and have adequate room for expansion. Tea companies claim that the new woven fabric bags allow hot water to flow through faster, and that the resulting flavor beats anything a paper bag can produce. Some tea companies call their tea bags "infusers", "pouches", or "sachets", further enhancing the image of a superior product.

The new generation of eco-friendly tea bags brings with it a perception of luxury, elegance and social responsibility. In addition to their natural materials, some bags are hand-sewn or pressure-sealed, rather than glued or stapled shut. Today's premium tea bags are filled with the same high-quality, long-leaf loose tea that has traditionally been available only in bulk form. We have come full circle in the quality of the tea contained in tea bags, with premium teas, like those distributed as samples in Thomas Sullivan's pouches, now available to the general tea-consuming public.

Tea bags have been elevated to a new level, in both the quality of the tea they contain and their packaging. Some tea bags are packaged and sold individually, taking on the appearance of an extravagantly wrapped gift. It is not unusual to open a gift box of tea bags and discover each bag in its own air-tight pouch. And there is usually detailed information on each tag about the origin and characteristics of the tea, as well as the recommended brewing method. 🍃

In Canada, the businessman Theodore Harding Estabrooks, realized that packaging individual cup quantities of tea in tea bags were a means of assuring consistent quality from cup to cup. Estabrooks' company, Red Rose Tea, introduced tea bags in 1929.

Opposite: Mariage Frères tea counter, Paris, France.

The Many Colors
of Tea

Walk into a teashop, or simply peruse the tea shelves in your local supermarket, and you will find yourself faced with teas of many "colors" and blends. Some can be defined precisely as tea, while others are concoctions made from herbs and plants; more correctly labeled "tisanes".

By its strictest definition, "tea" comes from the leaves and buds of the tea plant *Camellia Sinensis* (a member of the camellia family), known in ancient times as *Thea Sinensis*.

Today tea drinkers tend to describe all infused beverages as tea, regardless of whether they are brewed from *Camellia Sinensis* or any other plant leaves. Tea purists may cringe when they hear a request for herbal tea or red tea because, strictly speaking, these are not teas.

Authentic tea is classified as black, blue, green, yellow, or white. Within these classifications, there are taste and quality variations. These result from factors such as the growing location and conditions, the climate, and the time of harvest. What all types of authentic tea have in common is that they start as leaves and buds from the *Camellia Sinensis* plant.

Once harvested or plucked, freshly-picked tea undergoes one or more processes before it is classified into one of the five color categories. These processes include: withering, rolling, oxidation, drying (desiccation), and grading (sorting). The tea master on a tea plantation determines which processes to conduct.

Withering

The first step that almost all tea leaves and buds undergo is withering. This is a way of softening the tea to make it pliable enough for further processing. White tea is withered for a short period of four or five hours, while other teas may be allowed to wither for as long as 24 hours. The longer the tea withers, the lower the moisture content of the leaves. Besides losing moisture during withering, the tea also undergoes a chemical reaction, in which the starch in the leaf starts converting to sugar. In the early days of tea drinking, tea was made by simply immersing fresh leaves in hot water. The result was very bitter, probably because the starch in the leaves had not begun to convert to sugar.

Rolling

After withering, the tea leaves are ready to be rolled, either by hand or machine. During this process, the leaves are slightly crushed, allowing them to release sap.

Oxidation

Controlled oxidation begins after the rolling process. (There is also some natural oxidation during the withering and rolling processes.) The rolled leaves are spread out in a cool and damp place, with air circulating over them, for several hours. During the chemical reaction of oxidation, which occurs when oxygen comes in contact with the leaves and the sap released during the rolling process, heat builds up. The tea master carefully monitors the temperature of the oxidizing leaves to achieve the desired taste of the tea. As the leaves oxidize, their color changes from green to coppery red and the flavor changes too.

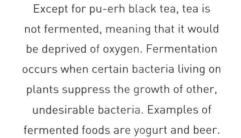

Except for pu-erh black tea, tea is not fermented, meaning that it would be deprived of oxygen. Fermentation occurs when certain bacteria living on plants suppress the growth of other, undesirable bacteria. Examples of fermented foods are yogurt and beer.

Oxidation generates thearubigins. These cause the leaves to change color, in the same way that a cut pear or avocado turns dark when exposed to air. Oxidation also produces theaflavins, which contribute to the flavor of the tea.

Drying

To stop the oxidation, the tea leaves are subjected to heat, with temperatures ranging from 130°F (54°C) to over 200°F (93°C). The drying process is quick, taking only 15 or 20 minutes. For optimal flavor and quality, the leaves are dried to a moisture content of 3–12 percent. During drying, the leaf color changes again, this time from copper shades to black or dark brown. Leaves with a moisture content of more than 12 percent can become moldy, and those with a lesser moisture content may lack flavor or have a burnt taste. A properly dried tea is a chemically stable and storable product.

Grading

The final stage in tea production is the grading or sorting. During this process, the leaf pieces are separated by size. They are classified as whole leaf, broken leaf, fannings, or dust. The larger the leaf piece, the higher the quality of tea. Some teas, such as black tea, undergo all five processes and are fully oxidized. Others, such as green tea, are not allowed to oxidize at all. The color describes the appearance of the dry tea and also, to some degree, the color that results after brewing.

Black Tea

While simply called "black tea", it is a blend of orange pekoe and pekoe cut black tea. Black tea is completely oxidized and processed during the withering, rolling,

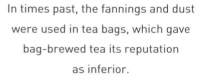

In times past, the fannings and dust were used in tea bags, which gave bag-brewed tea its reputation as inferior.

Opposite: Top left to right: Yellow tea, Black tea, White tea. Bottom: left to right: Blue tea, Green tea.

oxidation, drying, and sorting stages. Pu-erh black tea, the only black tea variety that is fermented, may or may not undergo oxidation. Today, most of it is loose-leaf after processing, but it can be compressed into tea "bricks". It is not unusual for high-quality pu-erh to age for thirty to fifty years. It is sometimes described as "living" tea because it contains microbes, or bacteria, and never stops changing due to its ongoing natural fermentation.

Blue Tea

Blue tea is more often called "oolong tea". It is halfway between green and black tea. Blue tea undergoes all five processing steps of withering, rolling, oxidation, drying, and sorting, but the oxidation step is only partial. The amount of oxidation depends on the method used to produce the blue tea. The two major methods are the Chinese and the Formosa methods. With the Chinese method, the leaves are 12–15 percent oxidized ; with the Formosa Method, the leaves are 60–70 percent oxidized, resulting in a tea very similar to black tea. Formosa tea, also known as "oriental beauty", is popular in Europe and the U.S.

Green Tea

Green tea is withered, rolled, and immediately dried. It is not oxidized. Green tea is often rolled more tightly than blue and black tea, sometimes so tightly that the leaves form tiny balls that unfurl when brewed. How green tea is dried depends on where it is processed. In China, it is usually roasted or pan fired over a flame, or tumble dried by blown heat. In warm, dry parts of China and India, green tea can be

"Pekoe" is a term used by tea producers to describe the leaf size of whole-leaf black tea. "Pekoe" comes from the Chinese *Pak-Ho*, meaning "hair" or "down", and refers to the fine, white down that covers the buds of the tea plant. Pekoe cut black tea has shorter, broken leaves.

Opposite: With baskets on their backs, harvesters pick tea leaves atop a hill in Norton Bridge, Ceylon, 2007.

dried naturally in the sun. In Japan, green tea is sweated in a steam tank and then hand-rolled. The sweating and rolling procedure is repeated several times, until the desired dryness is achieved. The drying method determines the flavor of the green tea; when it is roasted or pan fired, it has a taste of citrus and smoke; when it is steamed, the taste is more herbaceous.

Yellow Tea

Yellow tea dates back to sixteenth century China, and, since very little yellow tea has ever been exported, the Chinese remain its primary consumers. Yellow tea is generally made from only the buds or tips of the tea plant. It must be hand-picked. Yellow tea, like green tea, is not allowed to oxidize. Unlike green tea, yellow tea is dried slowly without the use of a heat source. While drying, the tea leaves are stacked up. There is some natural oxidation, and the polyphenols in the leaves cause them to change color from green to yellow. Yellow tea goes directly from picking to drying. It has a sweeter, less grassy taste than green tea.

White Tea

White tea is similar to yellow tea in its processing and its source. It is either air- or flame-dried, without being allowed to wither. Unlike yellow tea, its leaves are not stacked during drying, which shortens the drying period. White tea takes on a silvery-white color that comes from the down remaining on the young leaves as they dry. When brewed, it is very pale in hue. ꕥ

Matcha is a powdered green tea produced in Japan. Matcha is gaining popularity throughout the world as a beverage and as an ingredient in prepared foods, such as baked goods and ice cream. To produce matcha, the tea is dried, sweated, and then chopped into tiny pieces. It then undergoes one last drying cycle and is finally ground into a powder by a millstone.

Opposite: Japanese farmer supervises his wife and daughter-in-law as they pick leaves from tea plants on his farm, 1952.

Tea Variations

Flowering Tea

Flowering teas, also called "blooming", "presentation", "display", or "artisan" teas, are growing in popularity. They are bundles of tea leaves, hand-sewn together to form a bud, flower, or other shape. Flower buds and other flavorings may be incorporated into the "flower". Tea flowers are fairly expensive because of the hand labor involved in their fabrication. They are usually made from high quality white, green, or black tea.

It is not certain when flowering teas were first fabricated. Some claim they date back to China 200 years ago, but were banned as frivolous during the Cultural Revolution. Others say that a Chinese farmer, while experimenting with sewing tea leaves and flower buds together, invented flowering tea about a decade ago.

Regardless of its origins, flowering tea caught on and has become popular as a beverage, gift, and conversation piece. Several tea companies sell flowering teas. The flower is brewed in a clear glass teapot or similar container. When it comes into contact with hot water, the tea flower unfolds, like a time-lapse photo of a real flower. Tea flowers can be re-steeped several times and kept moist as a decorative item. Flowering tea is best shared with others since it is not only tasty, but also a conversation piece. It's also a wonderful means of slowing down our fast-paced lives a little.

Bubble Tea

Bubble tea, also called "boba," is a tea drink made with sweetened tapioca pearls and optional flavorings. (The Preparing Tea and Tisanes chapter contains two recipes for bubble tea.)

Bubble tea as a popular drink is said to have originated in Taiwan in the 1980s. Bubble tea cafés are now found throughout the world, particularly in areas with large Asian populations. Bubble tea cafés are popular in Canada, the U.S. (particularly on the East and West coasts), Australia, and South and Central America. Of course, they continue to flourish in Asia.

The original Taiwanese version of bubble tea was made with hot black tea, large pearl tapioca, condensed milk, and honey. As it became part of popular culture, creative variations of the drink have evolved. Bubble tea is prepared iced or hot, with fruit flavorings or juices, and with or without milk. Hot or cold, it is drunk through a straw. The tapioca pearls are slurped up while the tea is sipped.

Today's bubble tea cafés are much like the also-popular juice bars. Bubble tea has made tea drinking a social activity, not only for adults but also for teens and younger people. Most cafés feature a large menu of bubble tea drinks and will also create special orders. Bubble tea cafés are lively informal gathering places, with music blaring, a stack of magazines and newspaper to read, and, often, free Internet access. Some also serve snacks and light meals. 🦋

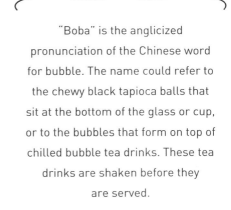

"Boba" is the anglicized pronunciation of the Chinese word for bubble. The name could refer to the chewy black tapioca balls that sit at the bottom of the glass or cup, or to the bubbles that form on top of chilled bubble tea drinks. These tea drinks are shaken before they are served.

Opposite: Macro image of tapioca pearls, the key ingredient in the popular bubble tea beverage.

Infusions and Tisanes

The five classifications of tea—black, blue, green, yellow, and white—are the only ones produced from the *Camellia Sinensis* plant. All other types of plant-based infusions are not considered authentic tea, but since they are consumed these days in the same manner as tea, they are usually referred to, and marketed as, tea.

Such beverages are more appropriately referred to as "herbal infusions" or "tisanes", but are just as likely to be called "herbal tea" on their packages and on restaurant menus. This inevitably leads to further discussion of the meaning of "herbal", since tea from the *Camellia Sinensis*, a botanical plant, can also be classified as herbal.

Ultimately, for those of us who enjoy the warm and cold beverages made from tea and other plants, the question of their authenticity as tea makes little difference. Our enjoyment is most important.

In addition to broadening the spectrum of tea flavors, tisanes are caffeine-free, making them an appropriate beverage choice for children and for those wishing to limit their caffeine consumption. One word of warning about tisanes, though: little is known about the effects of drinking tisanes. Although they are "natural" and caffeine-free, some plants can cause physical side effects. Some tisanes that have achieved worldwide popularity are rooibos, yerba mate (pronounced "matay") and, to a lesser extent, honeybush.

Opposite: Top left to right: Mint, Rosehip, Chamomile.
Bottom: left to right: Ginseng, Yerba Mate, Rooibos

Rooibos and Honeybush

Rooibos (pronounced roy-boss) is a caffeine-free herbal beverage produced from the needle-shaped leaves and stems of the rooibos bush, which is native to South Africa. "Rooibos" means "red bush" in Afrikaans. The plant's botanical name is *Aspalathus Linearis*. South Africans from the Cedarberg Mountain region, where the bush grows, have been drinking rooibos for over three hundred years.

Rooibos, often called "red tea" or "red bush tea", is flavorful and naturally sweet. It also earns points for being low in caffeine and high in antioxidants. The versions processed for worldwide consumption are usually oxidized and brew to a deep red hue.

Another South African red tea is honeybush. It is similar in appearance and flavor to rooibos, only a bit sweeter. Its honey flavor comes from the sweet scent of the honeybush flowers. The honeybush plant (*Cyclopia Intermedia*) grows in the mountains of the Longkloof District in the Eastern Cape.

Yerba mate

Yerba mate is an infusion made from the dried leaves of the *Ilex paraguariensis* tree, the evergreen South American holly tree. It is the national drink of Argentina, Paraguay, and Uruguay. Yerba mate has been drunk by the indigenous people of South America since as early as the fifteenth century.

In contrast to rooibos, with its calming effect and lack of caffeine, yerba mate is sought after for its stimulating effect. It has a smokey flavor. Though scientists are still uncertain about the amount of caffeine it contains, they do acknowledge its caffeine-like effect.

Endless Other Options for Herbal Infusions anTisanes

In today's marketplace, there is no limit to the number of teas made from plants other than the *Camellia Sinensis*. Just about any edible plant can be made into an herbal tea.

Chamomile, mint, lavender, lemon myrtle, dried fruits and berries, ginseng, hibiscus, rosehips, and lemon grass are just some of the plants that are brewed as infusions. Most commercial herbal teas are processed in a manner similar to green tea. Homemade herbal teas are just as likely to be made with fresh plant leaves as with dried leaves. ❦

The traditional way to drink yerba mate is from a gourd, called a mate. The dried leaves are steeped in hot water and drunk from the gourd through a metal straw, called a bombilla. The bombilla has holes in it to let the brewed liquid pass through while filtering out the steeped yerba mate leaves.

Buying and Storing Tea

Where to buy tea is the easy part. The challenge is deciding what kind of tea to buy. To address the easy part first, tea is sold in just about any store that sells packaged food-from large supermarket chain stores to corner Mom & Pop groceries. Most metropolitan areas have shops specializing in tea. Many coffee shops and cafés sell a variety of teas as well. Most tea companies sell their teas online in addition to their retail distribution.

The real challenge, then, is choosing from the many varieties and blends available. It is not unusual to find an entire supermarket aisle stocked with packaged tea. A teashop in the Chinese or Japanese district of any major city will typically be stocked floor to ceiling with canisters of loose tea.

Those of us who drink tea throughout the day often switch types depending on the hour and the occasion. Tea connoisseurs seek out specific vintages and seasonal harvests.

Blended teas further complicate tea choices. More often than not, tea is mixed with other ingredients or is an amalgam of several different kinds of tea: black tea with ginger; green tea with lemongrass and spearmint; green tea with jasmine blossoms; yerba mate with lemongrass and spearmint; chamomile with lemon balm, etc.

So, selecting tea for purchase can be as easy as picking up a package of your favorite at your local market or as involved as consulting with a tea merchant for recommendations of teas from around the world that might match your taste preferences.

In addition to selling loose tea or tea bags for brewing, many tea companies sell brewed tea in cans or bottles. While sugary tea in cans or bottles has been available for some time, pure ready-to-drink brewed tea beverages, made from tea leaves, pure water, and natural flavorings, are also common today.

Tea should be stored in an airtight container, at a constant room temperature, and away from natural light. It is best to use tea within a year of purchase. Oxidized teas such as black and blue teas have a longer shelf life than unoxidized green, white, and yellow teas. Herbal teas are best consumed within six months of purchase; with longer storage, they lose their flavor in the same way that dried herbs for culinary use do. Tea bags in individual sealed packages will have a longer shelf life than unwrapped bags in a box. ✳

Why does tea that has been brewed for longer than five minutes seem less stimulating? One theory is that longer steeping releases other elements into the tea as well. These elements may prevent caffeine absorption, resulting in a calming effect. One component of tea, the amino acid theanine, is known to reduce tension and stress without impeding alertness.

To Caf or DeCaf?

On average, an eight-ounce cup of tea contains between 10 and 60 mg of caffeine. A comparable cup of coffee contains 80 to 120 mg of caffeine.

The stimulant in tea is theine, which has the same chemical composition as caffeine and is generally referred to as caffeine. Tea can be processed to remove it. Herbal infusions or tisanes contain no caffeine, but may have other components that produce the same stimulating effects.

There are even subtle differences in the amount of caffeine extracted when tea is brewed. Generally, a tea's optimal brewing time and the amount of caffeine in a brewed cup will be indicated on the package. While these numbers are of some value, the actual amount of caffeine will vary with the size of the cup and the temperature of the water. Tea brewed in water that is hotter than the recommended brewing temperature will release more caffeine; tea brewed in cooler water will release less caffeine. Also, the longer tea steeps, the slower the rate of caffeine release. Lighter, unoxidized teas, for instance, are usually brewed for a shorter time than oxidized teas. Re-steeped tea is often described as milder, probably because there is less remaining caffeine to be extracted with each re-steeping.

By weight, tea contains more caffeine than coffee, possibly twice as much. However, a smaller amount of tea than coffee is needed to brew a cup. One pound of dry tea can make approximately 200 cups, while one pound of coffee yields no more than 60 cups. A cup of tea, more diluted than a cup of coffee, contains significantly less caffeine.

While many tea companies now indicate caffeine content on each package, there are too many variables in the brewing process to be certain of the actual amount of caffeine in a brewed cup. Furthermore, people metabolize caffeine in different ways, and a single individual's metabolism may vary, depending on the amount and type of tea or other beverages they consume, their health condition, and numerous other factors.

Decaffeinated Tea

Tea that is labeled as "decaffeinated" must, by law, have at least 97 percent of its caffeine removed. Tea drinkers who dunk regular tea bags for thirty seconds to a minute, believing they are reducing the amount of caffeine in their tea, do not achieve the desired effect because most of the caffeine is released right at the start of brewing.

One way to decaffeinate tea "naturally" is to steep it, either in a tea bag or loose, for 30 seconds to a minute. Then pour out the water and continue to steep with fresh hot water. Since caffeine is highly soluble in water, much of it will be eliminated in the first quick steeping. Commercial decaffeination uses ethyl acetate, methylene chloride, or carbon dioxide. The ethyl acetate and methylene chloride methods remove the caffeine, but can also remove the healthful compounds in the tea. 🐾

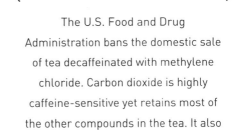

The U.S. Food and Drug Administration bans the domestic sale of tea decaffeinated with methylene chloride. Carbon dioxide is highly caffeine-sensitive yet retains most of the other compounds in the tea. It also leaves no residue and is considered the most natural commercial decaffeinating method.

Health Benefits of Tea
and Tisanes

A major reason for the popularity of tea is its health benefits. While tea has been considered a healthful beverage since its legendary discovery by Chinese Emperor Shen-Nung over 5000 years ago, modern science is still identifying the beneficial substances contained in tea. Whether tea's benefits are real or perceived, there is some evidence to substantiate its positive effect on health. To date, no credible research has revealed evidence that either tea or tisanes prevent disease.

Mixed Reports for Tea

Tea contains natural antioxidants called flavonoids, which are an important part of a healthy diet. Tea also contains energizing caffeine. Green tea is currently marketed, despite the lack of medically substantiated evidence, as the cure-all for almost any ailment. It is an ingredient in soaps, perfumes, toothpaste, juices, body lotions, and creams. It is sold as a food supplement and touted as an aid to weight loss. My guess is that the amount of green tea in beauty products is negligible. As for food supplements and weight-loss teas, I advise caution and recommend consultation with a medical professional before use.

According to one theory, the minimal processing of green, and possibly white, tea produces more antioxidants than are contained in fully oxidized black tea. Again, there is insufficient evidence to support this theory. Because tea comes from locations around the world with different climates and growing conditions, it is difficult, if not impossible, to make a generalized analysis of its components. Each sample may vary with testing. Even the amount of caffeine depends on the part of the plant sampled and the method used for brewing. For those people who do not have to limit their caffeine consumption for health reasons, the amount of caffeine in about five cups of tea is considered safe.

Tisanes: The Ultimate Cure-all?

The health benefits of tisanes, or herbal infusions, are usually described in terms of their curative or calming effects. The medical community continues to debate the validity of these claims. However, they agree that the lack of caffeine in tisanes makes these beverages a desirable alternative to coffee, tea, and other caffeinated beverages for those who wish to limit their caffeine intake.

This is a list of some of the more popular tisanes and their presumed health benefits:

Chamomile tea is best known for its calming effect and is often blended with other herbs and packaged as a bedtime tea. It is said to reduce anxiety, which helps to promote sleep. Chamomile tea is also believed to relieve menstrual cramps, aid digestion, and possibly aid in the management of diabetes and hyperglycemia.

Ginseng has long been considered an aphrodisiac. It is also thought to improve the circulatory system and sharpen mental functioning. Some rely on it as a general cure-all for everything from depression to hair loss to high blood pressure.

The longer tea brews, the less caffeine is released. More than 50 percent of the caffeine in tea is released in the first thirty seconds of brewing. One general rule of thumb: Since so little is known about the effects of drinking herb-derived beverages, it is best to consume them in moderation and with caution. Identify the source of the herbs first.

Hibiscus tea is believed to help lower blood pressure and cholesterol levels. It contains vitamin C, which may boost the immune system.

Lavender tea may relieve stress and migraine headaches, as well as aid digestion. Its calming effect may encourage sleep. Some use lavender tea as a mouthwash to eliminate bad breath.

Lemon grass tea is said to reduce stress, aid digestion in children, ease menstrual cramps, reduce fever, and have antioxidant properties. Lemon grass is often blended with chamomile and lemon myrtle, which both act as flavor enhancers and supplement the presumed health benefits.

Lemon myrtle is thought to have an anti-inflammatory effect, thus easing arthritis symptoms. It also has a calming, stress-reducing effect.

Mint tea is believed to relieve irritable bowel syndrome, nausea, vomiting, diarrhea, headaches, and infant colic. Its mint flavor may mask bad breath. The intense, refreshing taste of mint tea has a psychological benefit that cannot be debated.

Rooibos and honeybush are said to relieve stomach ulcers, nausea, constipation, heartburn, cramps, colic, and insomnia. These teas are believed to be rich in antioxidants. When applied directly to the skin, they may relieve itching, sunburn, and diaper rash. Their mineral content, which includes potassium, calcium, magnesium, iron, copper and zinc, can contribute to a healthful diet and overall good health.

Rosehip tea is high in vitamin C and also contains vitamins A, D, and E. Rosehips are often blended with hibiscus in teas. Rosehip tea is used to prevent bladder infections and relieve headaches and dizziness. It is said to be rich in iron and to help restore beneficial bacteria in the digestive system after a round of antibiotics.

Yerba mate is becoming popular worldwide because of its stimulating effect, which some perceive as sharpened mental clarity. Though experts still debate the caffeine content of yerba mate, they generally agree that it does not produce the less desirable effects of caffeine, such as jitteriness, often experienced after drinking highly-caffeinated beverages like coffee and soft drinks.

What facts do we know about the health benefits of tea and tisanes?

• They have no calories, when drunk without milk or sugar.
• Their natural antioxidants are similar to those contained in fresh fruits and vegetables and they are considered healthful.
• As beverages, they keep us hydrated and quench thirst. 🍃

PREPARING
TEA & TISANES

· · ○ ○ ○ · ·

Water and Water Temperature

A general guideline for brewing tea is to bring water to a boil, let it stand for a few minutes, and then pour it over the tea, allowing the tea to steep for three to five minutes, until it attains your preferred flavor and color. Blue, or oolong, and white tea often require longer brewing times to assure the desired flavor. Whole-leaf teas are brewed longer than broken teas.

Tisanes brewed from dried herbs are usually steeped five to ten minutes, depending on the herb. Tisanes made from fresh herbs should steep even longer to extract their full flavor and beneficial health properties. Berry and root tisanes are best prepared by simmering the chopped or crushed ingredients for 15 to 30 minutes.

Most packaged tea and tisanes carry recommended brewing instructions, as do loose tea and herbs, especially those purchased in teashops.

The most important element in preparing tea is the water. To showcase the flavor of brewed tea, use pure water that is free of minerals that could alter and compete with the taste of the tea. If the available tap water is not "neutral," use bottled or filtered water to brew the perfect cup of tea.

The ideal water temperature for brewing black and blue teas is in the range of 203° to 208°F (95° to 98°C) and, for green, yellow, and white teas, 158°F (70°C). Water that is too hot will damage the tea leaves and detract from the aroma and flavor of the brewed tea.

In reality, most of us do not carry a thermometer around with us to determine the temperature of the water when we make a cup or pot of tea. This is why I recommend waiting about two minutes after the water boils to add it to dark teas, and a few more minutes to start brewing light teas.

Once the tea is brewed, remove it from the cup or pot and serve.

To brew tisanes from dried herbs, either loose or in tea bags, use the water temperature recommended for green, yellow, and white teas. When brewing a tisane from fresh herbs, pour nearly boiling water directly over the fresh leaves.

How Much Tea
Per Cup?

If the vessel you use for brewing is made of porous material, it is best to use that pot or cup exclusively for brewing tea, preferably just one kind of tea, since the vessel will retain the flavor of the tea. Glass teapots are good for flavored teas because they do not retain aromas and flavors. Porcelain, china, and enameled cast iron are other neutral materials that will enhance the flavor of the tea.

For loose tea, use about a level teaspoon of tea for each 6- to 8-ounce cup of tea. If you place loose tea in an infuser or tea ball, use enough tea to fill it half full. This will allow the tea to expand and release its flavor when it comes in contact with the water. Use one tea bag per cup of hot tea. In general, let your taste be your guide and modify the amount of tea to suit your personal preference.

When brewing iced tea, use twice as much loose tea, or two tea bags, per cup of tea.

Use one to two teaspoons of dried herbs for each cup of water. If brewing from fresh herbs, use twice as much per cup.

For best results, preheat your teapot or cup by rinsing it with boiling water before adding the tea and hot water. 🍃

Re-steeping

An expert at a teashop in San Francisco's Chinatown agreed that tea, if properly stored in the refrigerator to prevent the growth of bacteria, could be re-steeped on another day, but that the quality would deteriorate with prolonged storage. She also had the following tip for achieving maximum enjoyment from tea: Use small cups, take small sips, and continue to add water to the teapot or cup to re-steep the tea and to keep it at the desired temperature.

Re-steeping is the process of re-brewing tea from the same tea leaves, one or more times. The resulting tea is usually as flavorful and satisfying as it was on the first brewing. Since premium and specialty teas, such as flowering tea, are expensive, re-steeping is one way to justify the splurge.

Loose tea and tea bags can be reused several times to prepare more cups or pots of tea. Each time the tea is re-steeped, it should be brewed a few minutes longer than the time before. Re-steeped tea is usually milder in taste and lower in caffeine, and it may exhibit flavor subtleties produced by new compounds released with each brewing. Some tea drinkers brew a pot of tea, pour the tea into cups or another heated pot, and then add more hot water to the tea to brew the next pot.

It is best to re-steep tea within a few hours, and no longer than one day, after the first brewing. Saving tea to re-steep on another day runs the risk of bacteria growing on the moist tea leaves. Refrigerating the tea inhibits the growth of new bacteria on the tea leaves; I suggest caution when doing this because any bacteria that started growing before refrigeration will not be destroyed and could even continue to grow.

Herbal infusions, tisanes, and other tea beverages can be successfully re-steeped if dried herbs are used. With fresh herbs, most of the flavor is extracted in the initial brewing; for optimal taste, do not re-steep fresh herbs. 🌿

Tea Drinks

One hot summer's day at the
St. Louis World Fair in 1904,
Richard Blechynden, Commissioner
of Tea for India and director of the
East Indian Pavilion at the Fair,
could not entice fairgoers to sample
his tea. In desperation, he poured in
some ice, creating one of the most
popular beverages at the
Fair—iced tea.

A few tips for successful preparation of tea drinks:

• Easily dissolvable sugar syrup, also called simple syrup, is the best solution for sweetening cold tea drinks. I also use it in hot tea drinks that require intense sweetening, such as Moroccan mint tea. Sugar syrup is easy to make and can be stored, and covered in the refrigerator almost indefinitely.

Basic sugar syrup recipe:

2 parts granulated sugar
1 part water

Place sugar and water in a pan. Stir. Heat to a low boil. Shake the pan and stir occasionally until the sugar is totally dissolved and the syrup is clear. Cool. Refrigerate in a closed container.

• Sugar or sugar syrup substitute: For those limiting their sugar intake, a natural alternative sweetener is agave nectar, sold in bottles at grocery and specialty food stores. The type I buy, "blue agave," is said to be sweeter but lower in calories than sugar and have a very low glycemic index. I've used agave in place of sugar syrup, with excellent results. I always use it to sweeten tapioca pearls for bubble tea. I think the flavor agave produces is more similar to sugar than any other sugar alternative.

• If you drink or serve iced tea often, keep tea ice cubes (made from your favorite tea) in the freezer and use them in your next batch. They will keep the tea from becoming diluted as the cubes melt.

Hot drinks

Moroccan Mint Tea

Makes 1 cup

Moroccans drink sweet mint tea throughout the day. It is a traditional symbol of hospitality, offered in homes, shops and other public places. Moroccan shopkeepers often invite customers to take a break and enjoy a glass of tea while they are shopping. By custom, the tea is poured into a small glass, usually filled halfway so that it is not too hot to hold at the top. The traditional teapot used for brewing mint tea is made of metal and has an extended spout. The tea is poured in a long stream, from a height of at least foot, into a small glass. This impressive ceremony is both festive and functional, since the extended pour also aerates the tea.

Fresh mint sprigs
1 teaspoon or tea bag of jasmine
  green tea per 8-ounce serving
1½ tablespoons sugar syrup per
  8-ounce serving

1. Wash mint and trim off long stems. Lightly crush mint in your hand and place in a warmed glass or small teapot. Add tea and sugar syrup. Pour in near-boiling water.

2. Steep for 3 to 4 minutes. Stir and strain into another warmed glass, if available. Pour from a height to create bubbly foam on top of glass. If brewing and drinking from the same glass, remove mint and tea before drinking.

3. Give a few quick stirs with a whisk or fork to aerate. Serve with a pitcher of sugar syrup for those who desire even more sweetness.

4. Re-steeping note: Fresh mint releases most of its flavor in the first steeping. If you want to make a second serving, add fresh mint and sugar syrup to the green tea.

Hot Milk Tea

Makes 1 cup

1 teaspoon or bag of black
   tea. Assam, English
   breakfast, and yunnan
   are good choices
Milk and sugar to taste

This simple tea is a popular breakfast or morning tea. Some also enjoy it as a mid-afternoon pick-me-up.

1. Warm the cup or teapot by rinsing it with hot water. Add tea.

2. Pour hot water over tea and allow to stand 3 to 5 minutes.

3. Stir tea and remove or strain out.

4. Add milk and sugar to taste.

Rooibos Latte

·······

Makes one 12-ounce cup or mug

8 ounces double-strength,
  hot-brewed rooibos
  (made with 2 teaspoons loose
  rooibos or 2 tea bags)
¼ teaspoon vanilla
Sugar to taste, optional
4 ounces steamed or heated milk
Whipped cream
Ground cinnamon, optional

Just about any kind of tea can be used to make a tea latte. I especially like rooibos because of its natural sweetness and lack of caffeine. I usually enjoy my lattes in the afternoon or evening, when I limit my caffeine intake. This is a wonderful after-dinner drink.

I. Pour brewed rooibos into warmed mug. Mix in vanilla and sugar.

2. Gently pour in heated milk.

3. Top with whipped cream and cinnamon.

Green Bubble Milk Tea

·······

Makes one 12-ounce glass

2 teaspoons or tea bags green tea

8 ounces hot water

2 ounces milk

¼ cup sweetened tapioca pearls (see opposite page)

1 wide straw, available at Chinese markets and online

Bubble tea is all the craze, especially in major cities and college towns, where bubble tea cafés are popular gathering places. This slightly sweet tea drink, with its tapioca pearls at the bottom of the glass or mug, is fun to drink. Bubble tea is sipped through a wide straw that rests at the bottom of the glass and draws in the pearls.

Preparing bubble tea at home requires some advance planning because the sweetened tapioca pearls must be cooked and sweetened first. Every few days, I cook up a batch of tapioca pearls and store them, covered, in the refrigerator, to have on hand for mixing into a glass of homemade bubble tea.

1. Heat milk to a simmer. Add hot water and tea.

2. Allow tea to brew in milk/water mixture about 3 minutes. Tea can be brewed in the same pot in which the milk is heated. Using a pot with a spout, or transferring the milk/hot water/tea to a measuring cup for the brewing, makes it easier to pour the mixture into the serving glass.

3. Pour tapioca pearls into bottom of serving glass. Add tea/milk mixture; pour through a strainer if using loose tea. Serve with a wide straw.

How to Cook Tapioca Pearls

1 cup black tapioca pearls (large
    diameter, dark color), available at
    Chinese markets and online
6 cups water

1. Bring water to boil in a pan. Stir in
tapioca pearls. When pearls float to
top of boiling water, cover pan and
boil gently for 20 to 25 minutes. Stir after
10 minutes to loosen pearls that may
stick together or to bottom of pan.
2. Test at 20 minutes to see if pearls
are soft and gummy, but not mushy.
Remove pan from heat and allow
pearls to rest in water, covered, for
another 25 minutes.
3. Drain pearls and rinse with cool water.
4. Transfer pearls to bowl and coat
with sugar syrup*, cover bowl, and
allow to rest another 25 minutes.
Pearls are ready for use or can be
stored in refrigerator for several days.

----

* NOTE: Agave nectar is an excellent
alternative to sugar syrup for
sweetening the tapioca pearls.

Matcha Latte

·······

Makes 1 cup

1 teaspoon matcha powder
8 ounces milk
Sugar or sugar syrup to taste
Whipped cream

For years I've enjoyed green tea ice cream, not knowing that its distinctive taste came from matcha, a Japanese powdered green tea. Today, drinks prepared with matcha are often featured at tea and coffee shops. Matcha powder is sold in many grocery stores and teashops, as well as online. A package of matcha powder may seem a bit expensive, but it will last a long time since only a small amount is used to prepare a single drink.

I enjoy this matcha latte on my mid-morning break. When I prepare it for friends, they are always fascinated by the ritual of whisking the matcha into the hot milk.

1. Heat milk to a simmer. Pour a small amount of milk into a cup.

2. Whisk in matcha powder.

3. Add remaining hot milk and sugar or syrup to taste.

4. Top with whipped cream and a sprinkling of matcha.

NOTE: I like to mix the matcha latte in a bowl or a glass measuring cup so that I have enough room for whisking with a small whisk or a fork. I then pour it into a warm glass mug or cup.

White Chocolate Latte

·······

Makes 1 cup

Many coffee shops offer a latte made with white chocolate. Since I prefer tea to coffee, I experimented with making a white chocolate latte tea and came up with this recipe. For my taste, the white chocolate and vanilla give it just the right amount of sweetness.

1 teaspoon or bag black tea

8 ounces milk

4 ounces half and half

2 tablespoons chopped white chocolate (white chocolate chips work well)

¼ teaspoon vanilla extract

Whipped cream

Ground cinnamon, optional

1. Heat milk and half and half to a simmer. Remove from heat. Add tea and steep for 5 minutes.

2. Stir in chocolate until melted and blended into tea mixture. (You may need to return mixture to low heat.)

3. Stir in vanilla. Pour into a warm cup.

4. Top with whipped cream. Sprinkle with ground cinnamon.

A Single Cup of Chai

·······

Traditional chai is spiced black tea with milk. The chai served in many tea and coffeeshops is made from a packaged liquid mix that is too sweet for my taste. My version of chai derives most of its sweetness from spices. It is quick and easy to prepare. Add as much sugar as needed to reach your desired sweetness level.

Makes 1 cup

1 rounded teaspoon or tea bag black
   tea (English breakfast or
   any other full-flavored black tea is a
   good choice)
2 whole cloves
2 whole black peppercorns
¼ teaspoon dried ginger
½ teaspoon ground cinnamon
1 cardamom pod, lightly crushed
1 whole star anise

1. Pour simmering water over the tea/spice mixture.

2. Steep 5 minutes, stir, and steep another 3 minutes. Strain.

3. Add a splash of milk and sugar to taste.

Lemongrass Olive Tea

Makes 1 cup

1 heaped teaspoon of the
lemongrass/olive mix
1 sprig fresh mint
8 ounces water

This is a mild, soothing tea that can be made with ingredients from your own garden. If you are not up to drying your own herbs, you can buy both dried lemongrass stalks and dried olive leaves in grocery stores or online. Mix equal parts dried lemongrass and dried olive leaves.

1. Bring water to a boil. Pour water over lemongrass, olive leaves, and mint.

2. Steep 5 minutes. Strain. Sweeten to taste.

Catnip Tea

Makes 1 cup

1 teaspoon dried catnip
½ teaspoon fennel seeds, slightly
crushed
8 ounces water
Sugar or honey to taste

Cats aren't the only ones who love catnip. Many people enjoy a cup of steaming catnip tea at the end of the day to help them unwind. It may be the perfect before-bed beverage. The fennel gives the tea a mild licorice flavor.

1. Bring water to a boil. Pour water over catnip and fennel seeds.

2. Steep 5 minutes. Strain. Sweeten to taste.

Peppermint Chocolate Tea

·······

I usually associate peppermint and chocolate with chocolate-covered mint cream candy. If peppermint patties could be liquidized and sipped from a cup, this is what they would taste like. It's a wonderful tea to enjoy with children.

Makes 1 cup

1 teaspoon dried peppermint leaves
   or peppermint tea bag
¾ cup water
¾ cup milk
2 tablespoons bittersweet or
   semisweet chocolate, chopped
Whipped cream, optional
Sugar, optional, for added sweetness

1. Bring water and milk just to a boil. Remove from heat. Add peppermint tea and steep 5 minutes.

2. Stir in chocolate until dissolved. Pour into a warm cup.

3. Top with whipped cream.

Spicy Apple Tea

·······

Makes 1 cup

Equal parts water and fresh
  apple cider* or bottled apple juice
1 spiced herb (rooibos) tea bag or
  1 teaspoon loose tea per 8-ounce
  serving

Hot spiced apple cider is a popular autumn and winter beverage. This tea features the flavor of apple cider or juice and the spiciness of rooibos.

I use caffeine-free Good Earth brand Original Sweet & Spicy ™ Herbal Tea. If a spiced herb tea is not available, use a rooibos or black tea of your choice and add a few cloves and a piece of star anise to the water/apple cider mix while heating and steeping.

1. Bring water/apple cider mixture to boil. Remove from heat.

2. Add tea and steep for 3 to 5 minutes. Remove tea bag or strain, if using loose tea.

3. Serve immediately. For added sweetness, add a cinnamon stick to each cup of tea.

----

* NOTE: In the U.S., apple cider is freshly pressed apple juice, often a blend of several apple varieties. Unpasteurized apple cider is usually sold directly from apple growers during the apple harvest season. It will start to ferment after a week or so, as its sugar turns to alcohol. Fermented apple cider is called "hard cider" in the U.S. Pasteurized apple cider, sold in grocery stores, is more shelf-stable, but it will start to ferment once it's opened. In England and Australia, fermented apple juice is called "apple cider". Apple juice and apple cider are technically the same; both 100 percent juice from the apple. Some manufacturers also process the juice to clarify it.

Cold drinks

Cranberry Bubble Tea Cooler

Makes one 8-ounce serving

4 ounces brewed black tea, room
temperature or chilled

4 ounces cranberry juice

2 ounces sweetened condensed milk

¼ cup sweetened tapioca pearls (see
page 81)

Bubble tea coolers are refreshing alternatives to fruit juice smoothies, with the added fun of sipping up the sweet tapioca pearls. Most bubble tea cafés make their coolers with fruit flavored powdered mixes. I prefer to make my own with my favorite juices. I find that tart cranberry juice and black tea combined with sweetened milk and tapioca pearls make a cooler with just the right amount of sweetness.

1. Combine all ingredients except tapioca pearls in cocktail shaker or closed container. Add ice.

2. Shake to combine and chill. Spoon tapioca pearls into a glass.

3. Strain mixed liquids into a tall glass or mug.

4. Serve with wide straw.

Matcha Breakfast Shake

······

Makes 1 serving

½ medium banana

1 tablespoon peanut butter

8 ounces cold milk

¾ teaspoon matcha powder

This is my favorite nourishing quick breakfast. It is tasty and filling—a complete meal in a glass! For those who have breakfast on the run, the shake can be prepared the night before and stored in the refrigerator. Just stir and sip.

I. Purée banana in a blender or food processor. Add peanut butter and blend together with banana.

2. Add milk and matcha powder and blend until all ingredients are mixed together.

3. Pour into a glass and enjoy.

Refrigerator Iced Tea

······

Makes 2 quarts

2 teaspoons or bags black tea

2 teaspoons or bags apricot tea

6 cups of water

This is another version of "Unsweet" Iced Tea in which the tea steeps in the refrigerator overnight. Experiment with different mixes of flavored and herbal teas. The apricot tea in this recipe adds natural sweetness.

I. Place all ingredients in a pitcher. Cover and refrigerate overnight.

2. Strain and serve. Serve with sugar syrup, for added sweetness.

Ginger Lime Green Tea Cooler

·······

Makes one 8-ounce serving

2 ounces ginger limeade recipe
6 ounces jasmine green tea,
   brewed double-strength and cooled
   to room temperature
   (can be brewed in advance and
   stored in refrigerator)

Ginger Limeade

**Makes approximately
16 ounces**

1 heaping tablespoon minced
   fresh ginger
⅓ cup sugar
2 cups water
½ cup fresh lime juice (4 to 6 limes)

I tasted my first ginger lime green tea cooler after an exhausting bicycle ride on a hot summer's day. I've spent many a day experimenting, trying to create the ginger lime tea cooler of my dreams, and this is what I came up with.

During the winter months, I serve this drink hot. I use the same proportions of ginger limeade and freshly-brewed jasmine green tea.

I. For each 8-ounce serving, mix tea and limeade together and pour over ice.

2. To keep flavor intense, use ice cubes made from the green tea and limeade.

I. Mix the, ginger, sugar, and 1 cup water in a small pan. Stir and heat to boiling. Simmer 4 minutes.

2. Strain and cool to room temperature. Add the remaining cup of water and the lime juice. Stir to mix.

3. Can be stored in refrigerator for several days.

Southern Sweet Iced Tea

....

In the southeastern U.S., people drink their iced tea ultra sweet. If sweet iced tea is not *your* cup of tea, be sure to ask for "unsweet" iced tea, wherever you order it. Otherwise, prepare yourself for sugar shock!

Makes 1 pitcher (2 quarts) of sweet ice tea

9 regular-size black tea bags or 3 family-size tea bags (also called ice tea bags; one family-size tea bag equals 3 or 4 regular bags)

8 cups cold water

¼ teaspoon baking soda

1½ cups sugar

Optional garnish: Lemon slices, mint sprigs

I. Bring 4 cups cold water to a boil. Reserve remaining 4 cups water.

2. Remove boiling water from heat. Add tea bags and baking soda and steep for 10 to 15 minutes.

3. Pour tea into serving pitcher. Stir in sugar.

4. Add remaining 4 cups of cold water to fill pitcher.

5. Serve in tall glasses filled with ice. Offer a pitcher of sugar syrup to those who desire added sweetness. Can be stored for several days in refrigerator.

NOTE: The baking soda is said to soften the flavor of the tannins released during the long steeping and to darken the color of the brewed tea. If the tea becomes cloudy in the refrigerator, add a small amount of boiling water just before serving.

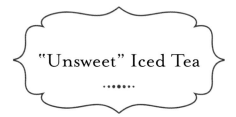

"Unsweet" Iced Tea

Makes one 8-ounce serving

2 black tea bags or
2 teaspoons loose tea
8 ounces cold water

This is the basic iced tea familiar to those outside the American southeast. It can, of course, be sweetened to taste. I usually make a pitcher of this tea and keep it in my refrigerator, covered, for a refreshing summer beverage.

1. Bring half the water to a boil. Remove from heat and add tea.

2. Steep for 5 to 6 minutes. Add remaining cold water.

3. Strain and serve in a glass, over ice.

4. Serve with lemon wedges and a pitcher of sugar syrup.

Dorothy's Brunch Tea

Makes one 8-ounce serving

1 part fresh squeezed orange juice
2 parts iced tea, brewed strong

Dorothy, the mother of a college friend, always served a pitcher of her "signature" iced tea when she entertained guests for brunch, including those from our college crowd. Now, many years later, I'd like to share her very easy recipe.

I still wonder if the adults in the crowd were adding vodka or rum to this tea. Worth a try, isn't it?

1. Mix the orange juice and iced tea. Chill. Serve as is, or over ice.

Thai Iced Tea

·······

Makes 2 quarts

1 cup loose Thai tea (available in most
Asian markets)
6 cups cold water
¾ cup sugar
1 can sweetened condensed milk
Fresh mint sprigs for garnish

Just about every Thai restaurant and some Vietnamese restaurants I visit serve Thai iced tea. It's easy to make at home if you have Thai tea. No other black tea results in the same spicy flavor and reddish-orange color.

1. Bring water to a boil. Remove from heat. Add tea. Steep for 5 minutes. (It will turn a red-orange color.)

2. Strain tea into another pot or a pitcher. Add sugar. Stir until dissolved.

3. Pour into an ice-filled glass until glass is about three-quarters full. Slowly pour condensed milk over tea. Let the milk float on the top or stir to blend in. Serve with straw. Garnish with sprig of mint.

NOTE: Black tea is the usual choice for iced tea. But don't be afraid to experiment with others, including rooibos and herbal blends.

Teagria

········

Makes 1 quart

Traditional sangria is a red wine punch made with fruit juice and fresh fruit. This non-alcoholic version is every bit as tasty. The rooibos gives it the same tint as red wine and adds a bit of sweetness. It is best made a day in advance. Serve it with your favorite Spanish and Mexican dishes. Pour it into the punch bowl to serve at a party or any festive occasion.

½ cup sugar

1 cup cold water

1 lime, sliced

1 orange, sliced

1 orange, cut in chunks

1 cup fresh strawberries, quartered

3 cups double-strength brewed rooibos

12 pomegranate, blueberry, or cranberry juice ice cubes

1 cup club soda

1. Dissolve sugar in water over medium heat. When sugar is completely dissolved, remove pan from heat and stir in lime and orange slices. Leave covered at room temperature for several hours.

2. Transfer mixture to a pitcher. Add orange and strawberry chunks and rooibos. Stir. Refrigerate overnight.

3. To serve, add juice ice cubes to pitcher and mix in club soda. Pour into tall glasses filled with a few regular ice cubes, adding more cubes as needed.

Mango Tea Smoothie

·······

Makes one 12–16-ounce serving

½ cup fresh or frozen mango chunks

½ cup coconut milk

½ cup pineapple juice

½ cup brewed white tea (one teaspoon or tea bag)

½ cup ice cubes

The tropical mango in this smoothie always evokes memories of my idyllic vacations in Hawaii, the Caribbean, and Tahiti. While mango trees grow in warm climates only, their fruit is available all year round in the markets of most metropolitan areas. If you can't find fresh mangoes, check the frozen fruit section in your supermarket for bags of mango chunks. For this drink, in fact, I prefer frozen mango. It saves me all that hard work of removing the flesh from the big pit. Besides, the icy mango makes this smoothie all the more refreshing.

1. Allow white tea to cool to room temperature or cooler.

2. Transfer to blender or food processor and blend with remaining ingredients.

3. Pour into tall glass.

Tea Cocktails

Spicy Apple Toddy

Makes 1 cup or mug

This variation on Spicy Apple Tea offers a bit more warmth and tranquility.

1. Prepare Spicy Apple Tea (page 89). Add 1 ounce brandy and stir.

2. Top with whipped cream.

3. Sit back and enjoy.

Green Tea Ni

Makes 1 glass

2 ounces vodka

1 ounce green tea, brewed double-strength (jasmine green tea or a tropical green tea blend are particularly good)

¾ ounce sweet and sour mix

This variation on the traditional vodka martini adds the flavor of floral green tea and a bit of sweetness.

1. Shake all ingredients in a cocktail shaker with ice. Shake until chilled and blended.

2. Strain into martini glass rimmed with sugar. Garnish with lemon slice.

NOTE: Suntory's Zen™ Green Tea Liquor can be substituted for the green tea and sweet and sour mix.

Cranberry Tea Spritzer

·······

When hosting a large cocktail party, I make my life easier by serving just one mixed drink. This festive tea-based cocktail is sure to be a hit at your parties. Prosecco, an Italian sparkling wine, is a tasty choice for this drink. A Sauvignon Blanc or Chablis works well as a still wine.

2 parts black tea, brewed
  double-strength
1 part sweetened cranberry juice
1 part sparkling or still white wine

1. Before the party, brew tea, bring to room temperature, and mix with cranberry juice.

2. Chill in pitcher or carafe, ready to pour.

3. At informal gatherings, I let my guests do their own pouring, adding a splash of wine if desired. For large gatherings, I serve the mix with the wine, in a punch bowl. I keep it cold by adding both black tea and cranberry juice ice cubes to the bowl.

Long Island Iced Tea, With Tea!

· · · ● ● ● · ·

Makes 1 serving

When I sip a Long Island iced tea, I have visions of a weekend of partying at a beach house. It's a great party drink for guests clad in Hawaiian shirts and flip-flops. Long Island iced tea is a potent cocktail that usually contains no tea. Its origin is unknown. Some say it goes back to Prohibition, when it was invented as an alcoholic drink disguised as a tall glass of iced tea. It would certainly have fooled the authorities back then. Others say the cocktail was invented in the late 1970s by a bartender named Robert (Rosebud) Buttu, who was working at the Oak Beach Inn in Long Island, New York. The concoction consisted of five white liquors, plus some sweet and sour mix.

No matter the origin, traditional Long Island iced tea does not include tea as an ingredient. The drink only looks like tea as a result of adding Coca Cola to the alcohol. I experimented with substituting black tea for the Coca Cola and am quite pleased with the results.

One word of caution: While this version of Long Island iced tea is tasty and a bit more diluted than the traditional version, I advise sipping it slowly and carefully. Its alcoholic content may take you by surprise.

Use a 1-ounce shot glass to measure the liquor

1 part silver vodka
1 part tequila
1 part white rum
1 part gin
1 part triple sec
1½ parts sweet and sour mix
3 parts iced black tea

I. Shake all ingredients, except the tea, in a cocktail shaker with ice. Shake until chilled and blended.

2. Strain into tall glass of ice. Add enough iced tea to give the drink the appearance of iced tea.

3. Garnish with wedge of lemon or lime. Sip slowly through a straw.

(*continued on next page*)

(continued from page 105)

Homemade Sweet and Sour Mix

Sweet and sour mix is sold in most liquor stores. It is easy to make at home too.

1 cup sugar

2 cups water

2 cups fresh lemon or lime juice.

1. Heat sugar and water until sugar dissolves (making sugar syrup). Add juice.

2. Stir and refrigerate.

Chamomile Grapefruit Gin Fizz

This variation on a gin fizz gets its fizz, and a bit of ginger flavor, from the ginger ale. I like the balance of the slightly tart grapefruit juice and the light, floral chamomile tea. Made in larger quantities, this refreshingly sweet iced tea cocktail makes a dazzling party punch. (See photo on opposite page.)

Makes 1 glass

4 ounces chilled chamomile tea

2 ounces pink grapefruit juice

1 ounce gin

1 tablespoon sugar syrup

4 ounces ginger ale

1. Mix all ingredients, except ginger ale, in a cocktail shaker with ice. Strain into highball glass, over a few ice cubes.

2. Fill glass with ginger ale and stir.

3. For party punch: mix all ingredients. except ginger ale, in a pitcher before pouring into punch bowl. Then add ginger ale.

Vodka Palmer

·······

Makes 1 glass

2 parts lemonade

1 part vodka

2 parts iced black, green, or white tea

Sugar syrup to taste

An Arnold Palmer, named after the golf legend, is simply a mix of equal parts iced tea and lemonade. This vodka variation on the classic drink promises relaxation after a day on the links.

1. Mix lemonade and vodka. Pour over ice. Slowly pour in iced tea. Sweeten to taste.

2. Garnish with lemon slice.

Green Painkiller

·······

Makes 1 glass

2 parts coconut rum

4 parts pineapple juice

1 part orange juice

1 part coconut milk or pina colada mix

Green tea ice cubes

Ground nutmeg and/or toasted
  coconut for garnish

I tasted my first painkiller many years ago, while sailing in the Caribbean. Over the years, I've tweaked the basic recipe to suit my personal taste. The addition of green tea ice cubes enhances the juice flavors.

1. Mix all ingredients except ice cubes and garnish in a pitcher. Chill.

2. To serve, fill glasses with green tea ice cubes. Pour juice/rum mix over the tea ice cubes.

3. To garnish, sprinkle each serving with ground nutmeg and/or toasted coconut.

Mint Tea Julep

....

Makes 1 tall glass

The mint julep, embedded in American Southern tradition, is "properly" drunk from a silver-plated mint julep cup—a small glass, only about four inches tall, with a three-inch top diameter, and resting on a base.

The mint julep is the beverage of choice at the Kentucky Derby. On Derby day, horseracing fans at Churchill Downs, and at bars and homes around the world, gather to cheer on their favorite thoroughbreds, while sipping a mint julep or two.

The addition of green tea to this classic cocktail lightens it up a bit without taking away its zip. Enjoy it while you watch the horse race or just relax on the front porch on a hot summer's day.

6 single mint leaves, plus 2 mint
  sprigs for garnish
1½ teaspoons sugar syrup
Crushed ice
4 ounces bourbon
2 ounces brewed green tea
2 slices lemon
½ teaspoon brandy

I. Muddle the 6 mint leaves in sugar syrup at the bottom of a highball glass.

2. Add crushed ice to fill glass about ¾ full. Pour in bourbon and green tea. Stir.

3. If time permits, place glass in refrigerator or freezer for about an hour to frost it.

4. Just before serving, add lemon slices, mint sprigs, and brandy. Serve with a straw.

Sake Tea

· · · · · · ·

Makes 1 tall glass

2 parts ginger limeade
3 parts light rum
3 parts iced green tea
1 part sake
Crystallized ginger for garnish

Sake has come a long way. This hot rice wine, once served only in thimble-like cups in Japanese restaurants, is now a popular cocktail ingredient in trendy lounges.

To honor the Asian origins of sake, I've used green tea and ginger, and have added rum and lime to provide a tropical dimension. I like to serve this version of sake with hors d'oeuvres at an afternoon party.

1. Mix all ingredients, except ginger, in a cocktail shaker with ice.

2. Strain over crushed ice.

3. Float a few pieces of crystallized ginger over the top.

TEA
SOCIALIZING

·······

Celebrating with Tea

Afternoon tea dates back to the second half of the seventeenth century. When Catherine of Braganza of Portugal married Charles II of England in 1662, she introduced the custom of afternoon tea drinking to the British. During that era, tea was a luxury of the upper classes and afternoon teas were often the time to receive guests. Initially, the occasion consisted merely of hot tea served from a pot, with guests adding milk and sugar to their liking.

It was not until the eighteenth century that afternoon tea evolved into a small meal between lunch and dinner, usually sandwiches and cakes to accompany the tea. Lady Anna, Duchess of Bedford, is believed to have started the custom. The light meal was known as low tea because it was served in drawing rooms on the lower level of wealthy homes. Low tea was also served on small low tables, similar to the cocktail or side tables in our modern living rooms. The wealthy dined late, so afternoon tea tided them over until dinner.

High tea, on the other hand, was the early evening repast of the lower classes, who worked hard from dawn to dusk. At the end of their day they needed a substantial meal. The high tea of those days, also called "meat tea", was the main meal of the day and included tea, meat, potatoes, eggs, cheese, bread, and other substantial foods. It was served at the dining table, where people of this class took all their meals. Similarly, today, we enjoy meals at our dining room or kitchen tables.

Nowadays, we generally use the term "high tea" to describe an afternoon cup of tea, accompanied by savories and sweets. Our high tea corresponds to what the

Opposite: Tea room at the Fairmont Empress, Victoria, British Columbia.

Opposite: Models Sue Davis (as Charmer), Mary Jane (as Butterfly), Sue Burgess (as Mascarade) and Ingrid Hepner (as Ice Maiden) pose for the camera during a 'Hatter's Tea Party', organized by the Millinery Institute of Great Britain and the London Tourist Board, 1967.

eighteenth century British knew as low tea. No matter what its label, the occasion is a special way of celebrating or simply spending time with friends. Personally, I prefer to call it "afternoon tea". Today it is enjoyed not only by the upper classes, but by people all over the world, from all walks of life.

Many large hotels in major cities serve afternoon tea. Tearooms, often a combination of teashop and restaurant, commonly serve afternoon tea, starting at mid-day and continuing throughout the afternoon. Among the world's legendary venues for afternoon tea are Mariage Frères in Paris, the Garden Court at the Palace Hotel in San Francisco, the Palm Court at the Ritz Hotel in London, the Russian Tea Room in New York, and the Fairmont Empress in Victoria, British Columbia. Tearooms are popular gathering places for groups (usually of women) who come to celebrate baby showers, wedding showers, birthdays, or other special events. Many cruise ships also serve a daily afternoon tea.

Tea cafés are more like coffee shops. In most, customers order their tea at the counter, whether for take-out or drinking on the spot. Some tea cafés also serve pastries and light meals. They are convenient places for informal meetings with friends and colleagues, and many provide internet access as well as newspapers and magazines for their customers. Bubble tea cafés are a currently popular type of tea café.

Making Your Own "Perfect" Tea Party

For decades, perhaps centuries, young girls have been hosting tea parties for their teddy bears and dolls. With their "friends" propped up in small chairs around a child-sized table, they sip tea and eat cookies, real or imaginary, from the tiny cups, saucers, and plates that make up their miniature tea sets. Of course, there is lots of conversation among the guests.

Even after the teddy bears and dolls have long been put in storage, tea parties remain an increasingly popular way to celebrate a special occasion or simply get together with friends for a leisurely visit.

A home tea party can be as simple or complicated, formal or informal, as you wish. Tea parties are meant to be relaxing get-togethers with lots of conversation, sweet and savory foods, and, lest I forget, tea. They can be luncheons, but are more traditionally mid-afternoon events. While in hotels or tearooms guests are served and are therefore confined to their tables, tea parties at home are always more relaxed and intimate. Guests can move around as they wish and linger over their tea.

A tea party provides a change of pace from our increasingly casual, yet frenetic, lives. It's an opportunity to dress up. Some guests might even don hats and gloves! It's also an occasion to polish the silver and dust off the fine china.

At a more formal, traditional afternoon tea food will include scones and clotted cream, tea sandwiches, miniature pastries and other sweets, and, of course, a pot of freshly brewed tea. For a more casual tea, the food menu is more flexible and can be decided by the host. Quiche, salad, cake and cookies are some of the possibilities. The tea, an essential component of the tea party, can be served iced, rather than hot, if the party takes place on a warm day.

There's no reason to feel intimidated by the idea of hosting a tea party. With specialty food shops and supermarkets offering a wide variety of prepared foods, you can purchase everything rather than prepare it from scratch. Many bakeries make miniature pastries and, if they don't, they will often accommodate a special order for smaller versions of their full-sized baked goods. If you do choose to rely on your own recipes, you can save yourself some work, and make your party even more of a social event, by inviting some of your guests to help assemble tea sandwiches, arrange food on serving platters, and brew tea.

Don't be shy about asking your guests for a loan of tea sets, serving pieces, or table linen. Most of us have special items we rarely use—an imported linen tablecloth, a sterling silver tea set, crystal water glasses, or bone china that has been in the family for generations. A tea party—your own or a friend's—is the perfect occasion to showcase these treasures.

Suggested menu for a home tea party:

....

Cranberry Orange Wheat Scones

Assorted Finger Sandwiches
Lemon Chive Chicken Salad
Chutney with Goat Cheese
Smoked Salmon

Chocolate Chip Lime Squares

Green Tea Madeleines

Marion's Dream Bars

Cranberry Orange Wheat Scones
•••••

The shredded wheat puts a new and healthful twist on the classic scone. (See photo on next page.)

Makes 24 mini scones

1 cup shredded wheat cereal, crushed
1½ cups flour
¼ cup sugar
½ cup dried cranberries
2 teaspoons grated orange peel
1 tablespoon baking powder
½ teaspoon salt
⅓ cup butter, room temperature
½ cup milk, plus 1 tablespoon
1 egg

I. Preheat oven to 425°F (218°C).

2. Mix shredded wheat, flour, sugar, cranberries, orange peel, baking powder, and salt in large bowl. Blend in butter. Mix by hand or with pastry blender until mixture is crumbly.

3. In another bowl, beat egg with ½ cup milk.

4. Add egg mixture to shredded wheat mixture. Stir until dough sticks together.

5. Knead dough 12 times on floured surface.

6. Divide dough into four parts, and make six balls out of each.

7. Place each dough ball on an ungreased baking sheet. Gently flatten to about ½-inch thick.

8. Brush tops of scones with remaining tablespoon of milk. Bake 20 minutes, until tops are golden. Serve with clotted cream and jam.

Finger Sandwiches

Lemon Chive Chicken Salad

I've enjoyed this tangy chicken salad, served on a bed of lettuce as a "meal salad", for years. Only recently, I discovered it also makes a tasty sandwich!

Makes 24 finger sandwiches

⅓ cup mayonnaise

12 thin slices whole wheat bread, crusts removed

1 tablespoon plain yogurt (nonfat or light yogurt are good low-calorie options)

2 teaspoons minced fresh chives

2 teaspoons fresh lemon juice

¼ teaspoon lemon zest, grated

Sugar

1 pound cooked chicken breasts, cut in ½ inch cubes

Salt

White pepper

Arugula or other spicy greens, about two handfuls

1. Mix together mayonnaise, yogurt, chives, lemon juice, lemon zest, and pinch of sugar in a bowl. Add chicken and mix. Add salt and white pepper to taste.

2. Lightly butter each slice of bread.

3. Spread the chicken salad on the buttered side of six slices of bread. Top with a thin layer of greens. Top with the remaining six slices of bread, buttered side down.

4. Slice each sandwich diagonally in both directions to create four triangle-shaped sandwiches.

5. To cook chicken breasts: Place 1 pound of deboned, skinless chicken breasts in a shallow pan. Pour over water and ½ cup lemon juice, cover and simmer for 10 minutes. Uncover the pan, remove from heat, and allow chicken to cool in the liquid for about 30 minutes.

6. Note: As a time saver, use leftover chicken breasts or buy pre-cooked chicken.

Chutney With Goat Cheese

······

The fruity chutney provides a sweet balance to the tangy goat cheese. The edges of this sturdy sandwich are easy to coat with chopped parsley.

Makes approximately 16 finger sandwiches

1 loaf dense white bread, sliced

4 ounces unsalted butter, at room temperature

8 ounces soft goat cheese

1 to 2 tablespoons heavy cream

1 jar fruit chutney (Major Grey's suggested)

1 bunch fresh parsley (the number of sprigs you can hold loosely in two hands), chopped

2-inch-diameter round cookie cutter

I. Using cookie cutter or rim of small empty can, cut 32 rounds of bread.

2. Butter one side of all bread rounds, reserving a small amount of butter.

3. Mix goat cheese with enough cream to make cheese easy to spread. Spread thin layer of goat cheese on each bread round.

4. Top 16 rounds with chutney. Cover with other 16 rounds.

5. Spread thin coating of butter around edges of each sandwich. Roll edges in chopped parsley to coat.

NOTE: The number of sandwiches will vary with the size of each bread slice. This recipe estimates two bread rounds per slice.

Smoked Salmon Sandwiches

·······

These cream cheese and smoked salmon sandwiches on thinly-sliced dark bread are far more elegant than the bagels with cream cheese and lox that I enjoyed for Sunday morning breakfast when I was growing up. The capers, dill and lemon provide some added "zing".

Makes 40 finger sandwiches

20 slices firm, thinly-sliced bread
   (rye or pumpernickel
   recommended)
1 cup cream cheese, whipped
½ cup small capers, drained
12 ounces thinly-sliced
   smoked salmon
1 bunch baby dill
1 lemon, quartered
Black pepper

I. Remove crusts from bread. Spread thin layer of cream cheese on each slice.

2. Sprinkle capers over 10 slices of bread. Divide up the smoked salmon and place each slice, on top of the capers. Squeeze small amount of lemon juice over each.

3. Place a sprig or two of dill on the salmon. Add black pepper to taste. Top with other pieces of bread. Slice into quarters.

Chocolate Chip Lime Squares

My husband adores lemon squares. I find them too sweet. I've tweaked his mother's recipe by substituting lime juice for lemon juice and adding chocolate chips. Yes, it's still very sweet, but I find the tart lime flavor offsets some of the sweetness.

Makes 16 to 20 squares

Crust

1 cup flour
¼ cup confectioners' sugar
½ cup melted butter

Filling

1 cup sugar
½ teaspoon baking powder
2 eggs, lightly beaten
2 tablespoons lime juice
Grated rind from one lime
  (about 2 teaspoons)
 ½ cup mini chocolate chips
Confectioners' sugar

I. Preheat oven to 350°F (177°C).

2. Mix flour, confectioners' sugar, and melted butter. Press into 8-inch square pan. (To prevent sticking, line pan first with foil or buttered parchment paper.) Bake for 20 minutes. Remove from oven.

3. While crust is baking, mix all filling ingredients except chocolate chips. Pour mixed ingredients over hot crust. Sprinkle chocolate chips evenly over top.

4. Bake for another 30 minutes, until filling is firm to touch. Remove from oven and cool for about half an hour. Chill in refrigerator. Cut into 1½- to 2-inch squares.

5. Sprinkle with confectioners' sugar before serving.

Green Tea Madeleines

**Makes 24 madeleines
(2 madeleine pans)**

⅔ cup sugar

1 cup + 1 tablespoon all-purpose flour

2 eggs, lightly beaten

5 ounces unsalted butter

½ teaspoon lemon juice

2½ teaspoons matcha powder

½ teaspoon vanilla extract

Confectioners' sugar

The madeleine is a tiny shell-shaped cake that originated in Commercy, France. It acquired its fame when Marcel Proust mentioned it in his novel, *Remembrance of Things Past*. In the book, the narrator dips a madeleine into a cup of tea and remembers events from his past.

Special madeleine pans, with a dozen shell-shaped indentations, are sold in cookware shops. If you don't have one, you can use a mini-muffin tin.
I first tasted a green tea madeleine in the restaurant of a Parisian teashop. When I ordered a bowl of matcha, one green tea madeleine was served with it.

1. Preheat oven to 375°F (190°C).

2. In a mixer, beat sugar and 1 cup flour with ¼ cup of beaten eggs. Melt butter in small pan until it browns slightly.

3. In small bowl, mix one tablespoon flour with 2 tablespoons brown butter. With pastry brush, lightly coat insides of madeleine molds or muffin tins. Cool remaining butter, while stirring, over bowl of cold water or ice. Mix cooled butter with flour mixture, remaining beaten eggs, lemon juice, matcha, and vanilla, until blended.

4. Spoon batter into madeleine molds or muffin tins, filling each about ⅔ full.

5. Bake about 15 minutes, until edges brown slightly. Test by sticking a toothpick or cake tester into center of one madeleine; if it comes out clean, the cakes are ready.

6. Invert madeleines onto baking rack to cool. Sprinkle with confectioners' sugar just before serving. If not serving immediately, do not dust with confectioners' sugar until serving time.

Marion's Dream Bars

When I got married, this was the one recipe of his mother's that my husband insisted I have. Many decades later, it is still his favorite dessert. It continues to be passed down through his entire family and is now being enjoyed by Marion's great-grandchildren, as I'm sure it will for many generations to come.

Makes about 30 bars

Crust
½ cup butter
½ cup brown sugar
1 cup flour

Topping
2 eggs
1 cup brown sugar
2 tablespoon flour
1½ teaspoons baking powder
¼ teaspoon salt
½ cup sweetened coconut
1 cup chopped walnuts
1 teaspoon vanilla

1. Prepare crust: Preheat oven to 350°F (177°C).

2. Blend butter, sugar and flour until they form dough. Pat into a 9 x 9-inch pan. Bake for 15 minutes or until slightly brown.

3. Cool to room temperature.

4. Prepare topping: Beat eggs lightly. Add brown sugar and beat well. Sift in the flour, baking powder, and salt. Stir to mix together.

5. Add coconut, walnuts and vanilla. Pour batter over baked crust.

6. Bake at 350°F for 30 minutes. Test with toothpick or cake tester in middle of pan. If it doesn't come out clean, continue baking for another 5 minutes, then test again. If the tester still doesn't come out clean, bake for a further 5 minutes.

Children's Tea Parties

At Christmas time, many hotels offer teddy bear teas for the younger crowd. Parents and their children, boys and girls alike, dress up and head downtown for a special afternoon tea. In many families the event is a tradition and grandparents often join in the festivities. Some restaurants and tearooms encourage children to bring their favorite teddy bear along; fancier and pricier venues may even distribute teddy bears as gifts to the young guests.

With slight revisions, the menu for an adults-only afternoon tea can be used for children at a Teddy Bear tea at home. Hot chocolate or tea diluted with lots of warm milk, peanut butter and jelly finger sandwiches, and bear-shaped cookies are just some of the things you could serve.

Of course, Teddy Bear teas are not strictly Christmas events. They can be enjoyed all year round to celebrate birthdays or other special occasions. The key to a successful at-home Teddy Bear tea menu is to keep it simple. Finger food is best.

Suggested menu for a teddy bear tea party at home:

Beverages
- Fruit Milk Tea
- Chilled apple or orange juice

Finger Sandwiches
- Peanut Butter and Strawberry Jelly

• Cream Cheese and Raisin

Sweets
• Fresh Strawberries and/or Grapes
• Fran's Brownies

The warm, fruit-flavored tea and milk will appeal to most children. The tea flavors I suggest are apricot, strawberry, or blueberry. Choose decaffeinated tea, if possible. Serve sugar cubes in a bowl with sugar tongs for a bit of elegance and a minimum of mess. Keep chilled fruit juice on hand for those guests who do not care for tea.

Prepare the sandwiches with sliced white or wheat bread. Remove the crusts first. Cut the assembled sandwiches into four triangles or use a teddy bear cookie cutter to make one or two bear shapes. Plan on two triangle sandwiches or one bear sandwich per guest.

When making the sandwiches, spread on only a thin layer of filling so that it doesn't ooze out. For the peanut butter and jelly sandwiches, spread one slice of bread with peanut butter and the other with jelly. For the cream cheese and raisin sandwiches, spread the cream cheese on one slice of bread, sprinkle with raisins, and top with another slice (that can be buttered first if desired). Close them up and cut into shapes.

For the sweets, I recommend any fresh fruit that can be eaten whole out of hand Strawberries and grapes are perfect. My brownie recipe came from a family friend, who has been making them for more than 50 years. It is still my favorite.

Another popular theme for a children's tea party is a mad hatter tea, inspired by the Mad Hatter in the Alice in Wonderland books. A mad hatter tea party should be an informal event, with lots of food, games, and, perhaps, a reading from Alice in Wonderland. Guests should be encouraged to wear crazy hats that they've made or decorated. You can also hold a "best hat" contest.

Fran's Brownies

·······

Makes 12 to 16 brownies

Fran's daughter always keeps a batch of these brownies in her freezer, just in case guests happen to drop by. Mine never last that long; I eat them frozen, right out of the freezer.

2 eggs

1½ cups sugar

1 cup flour

3 ounces semisweet chocolate

4 ounces unsalted butter

½ cup coarsely chopped walnuts or
  pecans (optional)

I. Preheat oven to 350°F (177°C).

2. Beat eggs. Add sugar and beat until smooth. Blend in flour. Melt chocolate with butter. Mix melted chocolate and butter thoroughly into batter. Stir in nuts.

3. Spoon mixture into greased 9 x 9-inch pan.

4. Bake for 30 minutes or until toothpick comes out clean after inserting it into the center of one brownie.

5. Cool brownies on a rack. Cut into small squares and serve.

6. Brownies can be baked several days in advance and frozen in an airtight container or bag.

Opposite: Ten-year-old Andrea Scholes, using the largest tea set in Britain, 1973.

BEYOND DRINKING
AND EATING

······

Skin, Hair, and Beauty

No matter where you purchase your beauty products, at a local drugstore or exclusive cosmetics shop, there is a good chance that green or white tea will be prominently listed among the ingredients. Is this merely smart marketing or an attempt to add health benefits to cosmetic treatment? There is no hard evidence that green tea perfumes or body lotions will give you a younger appearance or help you fight off disease.

Toothpaste companies are adding green tea extract, claiming that it prevents oral plaque and bacteria. Green tea is being used in breath mints, chewing gum, mouthwash, and dental floss. Here, too, evidence has yet to be found for the health benefits advertised by the manufacturers.

Tea Bag Art

Opposite: Original T-Bag art made with used tea bags.

One unique, alternative use for tea was developed in Cape Town, South Africa. Original T-Bag Designs is a collaboration of artists living in Imizamo Yethu, an informal settlement in Hout Bay. Money earned from the sale of the artists' work helps to support the community. Original T-Bag Designs receives donations of used tea bags from around the world and transforms them into works of art. The artists empty and iron out the bags, and then paint small, original designs onto them. No two art pieces are identical; the artists develop their own unique designs. The painted, recycled tea

bags are then used as decorative elements in a variety of items, such as greeting cards, gift bags, lacquered boxes, glass coasters, candle holders, and journals.

Jill Heyes, a British elementary school art teacher who moved to South Africa with her family, founded the company in 2000. What began as a small, cottage industry, showcasing the work of local women learning this special craft, has blossomed into a full-time business that sells the artwork worldwide. Original T-Bag Designs has not only provided local residents with employment and a steady income. It has also taught them a craft and given them a sense of accomplishment.

If you visit Cape Town, look for the Original T-Bag Designs shop in the Blue Shed, a craft market on the Victoria and Alfred Waterfront. Visitors are also welcome to tour the production facility in Hout Bay and to relax there over a cup of tea.

Original T-Bag Designs has marketing representatives in Canada, New Zealand, Germany, the U.S., Britain, Holland, and Switzerland. Check the company website for information on purchase locations and procedures for donating used tea bags. Original T-Bag Designs is supported by a major American tea company, as well as by organizations and community groups around the world. 🍃

Other Uses for Tea

Apart from drinking it, tea has many other uses. These are some that I've come across. They're certainly worth a try.

• Forget the fake spray tan! Dab your skin with tea instead to give the effect of a suntan. In the 1940s, women used tea to stain their legs when nylon stockings were scarce.

• Apply a wet tea bag to razor burns to ease pain.

• Place lukewarm tea bags on your eyelids to refresh tired eyes and reduce puffiness.

• Use a tea bag soaked in cool water to stop bleeding, relieve the sting of an injection, or alleviate the pain of sunburn.

• Use a soft cloth dipped in freshly-brewed tea to shine wooden furniture.

• Before filling a planter pot, place a few used tea bags on the drainage layer at the bottom. These add nutrients to the plant.

• Add a few cups of brewed tea to your compost pile to accelerate decomposition and create an acid-rich mixture.

• Repel mosquitoes by burning tea leaves in a room.

RESOURCES

Books and Articles

Heiss, Mary Lou, and Robert J. Heiss. The Story of Tea: A Cultural History and Drinking Guide. Berkeley/Toronto: Ten Speed Press, 2007.

Hohenegger, Beatrice. Liquid Jade: The Story of Tea from East to West. New York: St. Martin's Press, 2006.

Mariage Frères: The French Art of Tea. France: Mariage Frères, 2006.

Martin, Laura C. Tea: The Drink that Changed the World. Tokyo/Rutland, Vermont/Singapore: Tuttle Publishing, 2007.

Okakura, Kakuzo. The Book of Tea. New York: Dover Publications, Inc., 1964.

Perry, Sara. The New Tea Book. San Francisco: Chronicle Books, 2001.

Online Resources

The Internet is a seemingly unlimited source of information about tea and tea culture. The following websites were particularly useful in my research. Note that most commercial tea company websites offer products for sale or refer visitors to retail outlets.

American Tea Masters Association
http://www.TeaMasters.org
Offers classroom and online training to become a Certified Tea Master™.
9115 Valencia St.
San Diego, California 91977 USA

Boba Tea Direct
http://www.bobateadirect.com
For ordering bubble tea supplies, including powder mixes, straws, and tapioca. Also several informative articles on bubble/boba tea.

Bubble Tea Supply
http://www.bubbleteasupply.com
Mail-order bubble tea supplies, including mixes, syrups, straws, and tapioca pearls.

Cargo and James
http://www.cargoandjames.com
Excellent guide to categories of tea and herbal infusions.

DoMatcha Tea
http://www.domatcha.com
Online mail orders for matcha and matcha accessories. The website describes the cultivation and use of matcha.

Fabricant, Florence, "Tea's Got a Brand New Bag." The New York Times (September 13, 2006).
http://www.nytimes.com/2006/09/13/dining/13tea.html

Good Earth Teas
http://goodearthteas.com
Information for direct or mail-order purchase in the U.S., Canada, and Britain. Informative FAQs.

Gomestic.com
http://www.gomestic.com
Helpful tips on preparing and using tea, not only as a beverage.

Ito En Tea Company
http://www.itoen.com
Manufacturer of premium bottled fresh tea. Useful guide to tea preparation and interesting account of tea history.

Lipton Tea
http://www.liptont.com
Good tea history and suggested uses for tea.

Lollicup
http://lollicup.com
Bubble tea supplies for online purchase.

Loving-Long-Island.com
http://www.loving-long-island.com/long-island-ice-tea-history-and-recipe.html
One person's account of the invention of Long Island iced tea.

Numi Tea
http://www.numitea.com
Includes an informative tea tutorial.

Organic Flavor Company
http://www.onefinecup.nl/en/default.asp
Informative FAQ section on tea and herbs.

Original T-Bag Designs
http://www.tbagdesigns.co.za
In South Africa, its tea bag art products are sold at the T-Bag Designs Waterfront Stall in the Blue Shed on the Victoria and Albert Waterfront. The website provides contact information for South Africa, Canada, New Zealand, Germany, the U.S. Britain, Holland, and Switzerland

PG Tips
http://www.pgtips.co.uk
A longtime popular brand of tea in Britain.

Pettigrew, Jane, "It's In The Bag," TeaInternational, March, 2007.
http://www.teaandcoffee.net/0307/tea.htm

Planet Tea
http://www.planet-tea.com
Practical, general information about tea, in understandable terms.

PubMed
http://www.ncbi.nlm.nih.gov/pubmed/18681440
Medical study: "Protective effects of dietary chamomile tea on diabetic complications."

Red Blossom Tea Company
http://redblossomtea.com
Detailed descriptions of each of its teas, along with instructions for brewing and recommended pots and cups.

Red Hat Society
http://www.redhatsociety.com
Official site of the Red Hat Society, an international organization of women who dress in red and purple and get together for tea and fun.

Red Rose Tea
http://www.redrosetea.com

Historic Canadian tea company.

Red Tea of Africa
http://redtea.com
Useful information about rooibos and honeybush.

Salada Tea Company
http://www.greentea.com
Historic American tea company originating in
Boston, Massachusetts.

San Francisco Zen Center, Green Gulch
http://www.sfzc.org/ggf
The center conducts Sunday Way of Tea
ceremonies, open to the public.

Tea Benefits
http://www.teabenefits.com/
A summary of the presumed health benefits of
many teas and tisanes.

Tea Forté
http://www.teaforte.com

Ten Ren Tea
http://www.tenrenusa.com

The Institute of Masters of Tea Arts
http://www.mastersoftea.org
Offers accreditation programs: Master of Tea Arts
Diploma, Certified Tea Master,
and Premier Tea Master.

The Tea FAQ: The Definitive Guide to Tea
http://www.theteafaq.com
Detailed information on many aspects of tea culture.

The Tea Man's Tea Talk
http://www.teatalk.com

Twinings of London
http://www.twinings.com
Worldwide tea company established in London over
300 years ago.

UK Tea Council: Tea 4 You: History of Tea
http://www.tea.co.uk/index.php?pgId=4
Overview of tea history.

Wikipedia

http://en.wikipedia.org/wiki/Category:Tea_culture
http://en.wikipedia.org/wiki/Tea_bag
Many tea-related topics are covered in detail on
these sites, with links to others.

Yerba Mate Café
http://www.yerbamatecafé.com/home.html
Detailed information about yerba mate.

Contact Information for Tearooms cited in Tea Socializing

The Fairmont Empress
721 Government Street
Victoria, British Columbia, Canada V8W1WS
Toll Free Canada/United States telephone:
1-866-540-4429
International Toll Free telephone 800-0441-1414
(add originating country code as a prefix to this
telephone number) Local Canada telephone:
250-384-8111

Mariage Frères
35, Rue Bourg Tibourg
75004 Paris, France +33 1 44 54 18 39

Palace Hotel
2 New Montgomery Street
San Francisco California 94105-0671
Direct telephone number for afternoon tea
reservations: 415-546-5089

The Ritz London
150 Piccadilly
London W1J 9BR
Direct telephone number for afternoon tea
reservations: +44 (0) 7300 2345

The Russian Tea Room
150 West 57th Street
New York, NY 10019
Reservations: 212-581-7100
Special Events: 212-333-2970
General Information: info@russiantearoomnyc.com

ACKNOWLEDGEMENTS

Photographs by:

Danya Weiner 8, 43, 49, 52, 68, 71, 75, 77, 81, 85
88, 93, 94, 99, 100, 104, 107, 110,
112, 119 123, 125, 128, 132, 136

Getty Images 15
Evening Standard 116
Gilbert M. Grosvenor/
National Geographic 45
Harold M. Lambert 32
Hulton Archive 26, 37
John Downing 5
Keystone 134
Luke Bagshaw 16
Margaret Bourke-White/
Time & Life Pictures 46
Michael S. Yamashita 12
Popperfoto 23
Thomas Holton 25

Fairmont Hotels & Resorts 29, 115

iStockphoto
Alex Bramwell 62
Ivan Ivanov 59
Nancy Kennedy 50
Robert Churchill 67
Wando Studios 56

Library of Congress 11, 19

Mariage Frères 39

National Railway Museum England/SSPL 30

RedCo Foods, Inc. 34

T-Bag Designs 139

INDEX